BETTY —
I READ SOME OF
THIS & IT MADE
ME LAUGH — — I
KNOW YOU NEED
SOME OF THAT
(LAUGHTER) SO
ENJOY! (GOOD
BATHROOM BOOK!)
PH

The Smartest, Funniest, Dumbest Things *Ever Said*

TOMLIN • IVY BAKER PRIEST • BRONSON ALCOTT • T. H. WHITE • LEWIS CARROLL • AYN RAND • RALPH WALDO E
OSEVELT • ABRAHAM LINCOLN • GEORGE ORWELL • WILLIAM SHAKESPEARE • HENRY WADSWORTH LO
QUENTIN CRISP • EZRA POUND • SOCRATES • GEORGE ORWELL • HENRI FRÉDÉRIC AMIEL • HONORÉ DE BALZA
TAYANA • JOSH BILLINGS • NORMAN COUSINS • SAMUEL BUTLER • ERMA BOMBECK • THOMAS PAINE • WILLIAM
PERICLES • ELIZABETH CADY STANTON • MOLIÈRE • SAINT AUGUSTINE • H. L. MENCKEN • HENRY DAVID THOREA
AKE • BOB DYLAN • HENRY DAVID THOREAU • CHARLES DICKENS • WILL ROGERS • OSCAR WILDE • MARK TWAIN
DHA • CHARLES BUKOWSKI • EPICURUS • JAPANESE PROVERB • SØREN KIERKEGAARD • GEORGE SANTAYANA •
CARL JUNG • SIR WALTER BESANT • FRANKLIN P. ADAMS • LILY TOMLIN • IVY BAKER PRIEST • BRONSON ALCOT
MUHAMMAD ALI • JOHN HENRY NEWMAN • EURIPIDES • ELEANOR ROOSEVELT • ABRAHAM LIN
EFFERSON DAVIS • RALPH WALDO EMERSON • JOHN MILTON • DANNY KAYE • QUENTIN CRISP • EZRA POUND • S
CHESTERTON • ROBERT LOUIS STEVENSON • SAMUEL BUTLER • GEORGE SANTAYANA • JOSH BILLINGS •
TAIRE • HENRIK IBSEN • PLUTARCH • ALEXANDER POPE • ELEANOR ROOSEVELT • PERICLES • ELIZABETH CADY S
LUTHER STANDING BEAR • ROBERTSON DAVIES • RAINER MARIA RILKE • EUBIE BLAKE • BOB DYLAN • HENRY
CHWEITZER • JOHANN WOLFGANG VON GOETHE • HENRY MILLER • DAG HAMMARSKJÖLD • BUDDHA • CHARLES
IGUEL DE CERVANTES • CARL SANDBURG • POPE JOHN XXIII • ALICE WALKER • BRUCE BARTON • CARL JUNG • S
ROLL • AYN RAND • RALPH WALDO EMERSON • E. B. WHITE • SIR WINSTON CHURCHILL • MUHAMMAD ALI • JOHN
ENRY WADSWORTH LONGFELLOW • ARISTOTLE • ANNA SEWELL • JEFFERSON DAVIS • RALPH WALDO EMERSON •
HONORÉ DE BALZAC • DALE CARNEGIE • JEAN ANOUILH • G. K. CHESTERTON • ROBERT LOUIS STEVENSON
THOMAS PAINE • WILLIAM LYON PHELPS • DEAN ACHESON • VOLTAIRE • HENRIK IBSEN • PLUTARCH • AL
CKEN • HENRY DAVID THOREAU • HARPER LEE • MILLICENT FENWICK • LUTHER STANDING BEAR • ROBERTSON
• OSCAR WILDE • MARK TWAIN • ALICE WALKER • ALBERT SCHWEITZER • JOHANN WOLFGANG VON GOETHE • HE
RKEGAARD • GEORGE SANTAYANA • MAITRI UPANISHADS • MIGUEL DE CERVANTES • CARL SANDBURG • POPE J
VY BAKER PRIEST • BRONSON ALCOTT • T. H. WHITE • LEWIS CARROLL • AYN RAND • RALPH WALDO EMERSON •
AHAM LINCOLN • GEORGE ORWELL • WILLIAM SHAKESPEARE • HENRY WADSWORTH LONGFELLOW • AR
A POUND • SOCRATES • GEORGE ORWELL • HENRI FRÉDÉRIC AMIEL • HONORÉ DE BALZAC • DALE CARNEGIE • JE
ORMAN COUSINS • SAMUEL BUTLER • ERMA BOMBECK • THOMAS PAINE • WILLIAM LYON PHELPS • DEAN
ADY STANTON • MOLIÈRE • SAINT AUGUSTINE • H. L. MENCKEN • HENRY DAVID THOREAU • HARPER LEE • MILL
ENRY DAVID THOREAU • CHARLES DICKENS • WILL ROGERS • OSCAR WILDE • MARK TWAIN • ALICE WALKER • AL
UKOWSKI • EPICURUS • JAPANESE PROVERB • SØREN KIERKEGAARD • GEORGE SANTAYANA • MAITRI UPANISHA
ALTER BESANT • FRANKLIN P. ADAMS • LILY TOMLIN • IVY BAKER PRIEST • BRONSON ALCOTT • T. H. WHITE • LI
ENRY NEWMAN • EURIPIDES • ELEANOR ROOSEVELT • ABRAHAM LINCOLN • GEORGE ORWELL • WILLIAM S
EMERSON • JOHN MILTON • DANNY KAYE • QUENTIN CRISP • EZRA POUND • SOCRATES • GEORGE ORWELL • H
VENSON • SAMUEL BUTLER • GEORGE SANTAYANA • JOSH BILLINGS • NORMAN COUSINS • SAMUEL BUTLER • ER
EXANDER POPE • ELEANOR ROOSEVELT • PERICLES • ELIZABETH CADY STANTON • MOLIÈRE • SAINT AUGUSTINE
DAVIES • RAINER MARIA RILKE • EUBIE BLAKE • BOB DYLAN • HENRY DAVID THOREAU • CHARLES DICKENS • WI
NRY MILLER • DAG HAMMARSKJÖLD • BUDDHA • CHARLES BUKOWSKI • EPICURUS • JAPANESE PROVERB • SØR
I • ALICE WALKER • BRUCE BARTON • CARL JUNG • SIR WALTER BESANT • FRANKLIN P. ADAMS • LILY TOMLIN • I
• SIR WINSTON CHURCHILL • MUHAMMAD ALI • JOHN HENRY NEWMAN • EURIPIDES • ELEANOR RO
STOTLE • ANNA SEWELL • JEFFERSON DAVIS • RALPH WALDO EMERSON • JOHN MILTON • DANNY KAYE • QUEN
EAN ANOUILH • G. K. CHESTERTON • ROBERT LOUIS STEVENSON • SAMUEL BUTLER • GEORGE SANTAYA
EAN ACHESON • VOLTAIRE • HENRIK IBSEN • PLUTARCH • ALEXANDER POPE • ELEANOR ROOSEVELT • PERICLE
ILLICENT FENWICK • LUTHER STANDING BEAR • ROBERTSON DAVIES • RAINER MARIA RILKE • EUBIE BLAKE • BO
ALBERT SCHWEITZER • JOHANN WOLFGANG VON GOETHE • HENRY MILLER • DAG HAMMARSKJÖLD • BUDD
UPANISHADS • MIGUEL DE CERVANTES • CARL SANDBURG • POPE JOHN XXIII • ALICE WALKER • BRUCE BARTON
TE • LEWIS CARROLL • AYN RAND • RALPH WALDO EMERSON • E. B. WHITE • SIR WINSTON CHURCHILL • MUHAM
HAKESPEARE • HENRY WADSWORTH LONGFELLOW • ARISTOTLE • ANNA SEWELL • JEFFERSON DAVIS • RALPH W
DÉRIC AMIEL • HONORÉ DE BALZAC • DALE CARNEGIE • JEAN ANOUILH • G. K. CHESTERTON • ROBERT L
MBECK • THOMAS PAINE • WILLIAM LYON PHELPS • DEAN ACHESON • VOLTAIRE • HENRIK IBSEN • PLUT
L. MENCKEN • HENRY DAVID THOREAU • HARPER LEE • MILLICENT FENWICK • LUTHER STANDING BEAR • ROB
ROGERS • OSCAR WILDE • MARK TWAIN • ALICE WALKER • ALBERT SCHWEITZER • JOHANN WOLFGANG VON GO
ØREN KIERKEGAARD • GEORGE SANTAYANA • MAITRI UPANISHADS • MIGUEL DE CERVANTES • CARL SANDBUR
OMLIN • IVY BAKER PRIEST • BRONSON ALCOTT • T. H. WHITE • LEWIS CARROLL • AYN RAND • RALPH WALD
OOSEVELT • ABRAHAM LINCOLN • GEORGE ORWELL • WILLIAM SHAKESPEARE • HENRY WADSWORTH LO

The
Smartest, Funniest, Dumbest Things
Ever Said

2,250 Quotable Quotes
Ripe with Wit, Wisdom,
and Wordplay

Reader's Digest

The Reader's Digest Association, Inc.
Pleasantville, NY/Montreal

Reader's Digest Home & Health Books

Editor in Chief . . . . Neil Wertheimer
Project Editor . . . . Elissa Altman
Creative Director . . . . Michele Laseau
Executive Managing Editor . . . . Donna Ruvituso

Associate Director, Prepress . . . . Douglas A. Croll
Manufacturing Director . . . . John L. Cassidy
Associate Marketing Director. . . . . Ted Hannan

The Reader's Digest Association, Inc.

President & Chief Executive Officer . . . . Mary G. Berner
President, Reader's Digest Community . . . . Lisa Sharples
President, Reader's Digest Media . . . . Dan Lagani
North American Chief Marketing Officer . . . . Lisa Karpinski

The material in this book originally appeared in the following books, all published by The Lyons Press:

1001 Smartest Things Ever Said Copyright ©2004 by Steven D. Price
1001 Funniest Things Ever Said Copyright ©2006 by Steven D. Price
1001 Dumbest Things Ever Said Copyright ©2004 by Steven D. Price
1001 Insults, Put-Downs, & Comebacks Copyright ©2005, 2007 by Steven D. Price
The Best Advice Ever Given Copyright ©2006 by Steven D. Price

The Smartest, Funniest, Dumbest Things Ever Said was compiled and published by The Reader's Digest Association, Inc., by permission of The Lyons Press/The Globe Pequot Press, Guilford, CT

Project Management and Product Development . . . . dix! Digital Prepress Inc.

Designed by Timothy J. Shaner, nightanddaydesign.biz

Illustration Copyright ©2010 by Charles Rekow

Compilation Copyright ©2010 by The Reader's Digest Association, Inc.

Library of Congress Data has been applied for.

ISBN 978-1-60652-963-8

Address any comments about *The Smartest, Dumbest, Funniest Things Ever Said* to:
The Reader's Digest Association, Inc., Editor in Chief, Books
Reader's Digest Road, Pleasantville, NY 10570-7000

To order copies of *The Smartest, Funniest Dumbest Things Ever Said*, call 1-800-846-2100.
Visit our online store at **rdstore.com**

Printed in the United States of America

3   5   7   9   10   8   6   4   2

US 6318/L-OP

Contents

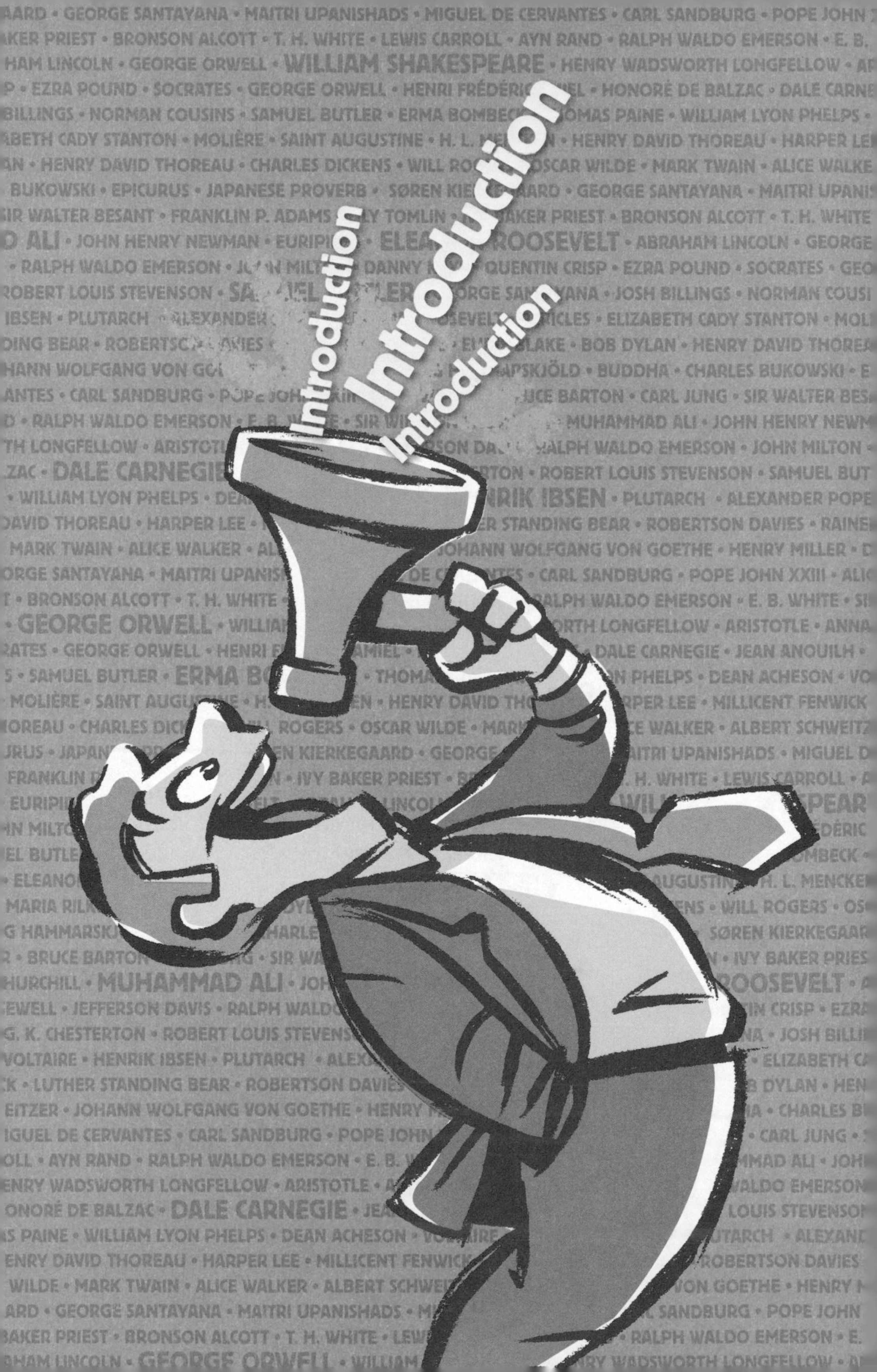

Introduction

We Americans use words almost every waking moment of our lives, but few of us know many details about the English language. The facts are plenty stunning though:

- The number of English words, if you include scientific and technical terms, totals about 1 million. That makes it by far the wordiest of the world's languages (by comparison, French has roughly 100,000 words).

- How did it get so big? Easy—by borrowing. Roughly 80 percent of English words are based on words from other languages.

- An estimated 750 million people speak English around the world. Of those, 350 million consider it their mother language.

- The average educated English-speaking person knows about 20,000 words.

- The typical person uses just 2,000 of those words in a week.

With so many people speaking so many words, you'd think most everything that could be said has been said. But the bulk of what we say is just the basic communications of everyday life. This hardly inspires us to be creative with our words—unless perhaps you are a parent seeking to describe new forms of punishment if your kids don't get to the dinner table *fast*.

> The power of words. . . . Put them together the right way, and you can lift a person's heart, guide her down a better path, make him laugh or cry or think. . .

But every now and then, people pull out of the air a handful of words and organize them in a way that has never been tried before. The results can be breathtaking. "Live simply, that others may simply live," said Gandhi—seven words that have layers and layers of meaning and beauty. At other times, it can be just plain funny, as when a famous politician uttered, "When your back's against the wall it's time to turn round and fight."

We at Reader's Digest certainly believe in the power of words. Put them together the right way, and you can lift a person's heart, guide her down a better path, make him laugh or cry or think, make someone feel they're on top of the world. We've been trying to do exactly those things for more than 80 years, and with *The Smartest, Dumbest, Funniest Things Ever Said*, we are proudly carrying on that tradition. The more than 2,000 quotes on the following pages are a wondrous mix of wise and weird, worldly and ridiculous, inspired and funny. It's read-out-loud entertainment of the first order.

Along the way, you'll encounter many of the world's greatest word masters. Some are comedians famous for using language as their playground. Some are renowned authors and thinkers who like Mark Twain, have a unique skill at telling the truth in fresh new ways. Then there are the politicians who flame (or douse) our hopes and ambitions using the wind power that is so much of political discourse. And on occasion, it's just a Hollywood starlet who has no clue how inane were the words she just said.

As we read the quotes inside, we wondered time and again how so little language could evoke so much emotion—or laughter. But that's the power of words. We hope you will enjoy them, share them widely, and use the wisdom and folly in this book to make your own life better.

The Editors

Part I
Smartest

Things *Ever Said*

What does it mean to be smart?
Is it wit or is it wisdom? Is it stylish
or is it sharp? Read on, and let these
wonderful words of wisdom inspire, stir,
and motivate you wherever you go, and
whatever you do.

Life can only be understood backwards; but it must be lived forwards.

—Søren Kierkegaard

Chapter 1

Life and Death

It's true: the only two things we can count on in life are death and taxes. But living well can also be the sweetest reward!

The future you shall know when it has come; before then forget it. —Aeschylus

· · · · · ·

One's own thought is one's world. What a person thinks is what he becomes. —Maitri Upanishads

There is no cure for birth and death save to enjoy the interval. —George Santayana

· · · · · ·

Time ripens all things; no man is born wise. —Miguel de Cervantes

· · · · · ·

A baby is God's opinion that life should go on. —Carl Sandburg

· · · · · ·

It is easier for a father to have children than for children to have a real father. —Pope John XXIII

The most important question in the world is, "Why is the child crying?"

—Alice Walker

· · · · ·

If you can give your son or daughter only one gift, let it be enthusiasm.

—Bruce Barton

· · · · ·

If there is anything we wish to change in the child, we should first examine it and see whether it is not something that could better be changed in ourselves. —Carl Jung

· · · · ·

I am afraid we must make the world honest before we can honestly say to our children that honesty is the best policy.

—Sir Walter Besant

· · · · ·

You can learn many things from children. How much patience you have, for instance. —Franklin P. Adams

· · · · ·

ACTING CHILDISH SEEMS TO COME NATURALLY, BUT ACTING LIKE AN ADULT, NO MATTER HOW OLD WE ARE, JUST DOESN'T COME EASY TO US.

—Lily Tomlin

My father always said there are four things a child needs: plenty of love, nourishing food, regular sleep, and lots of soap and water. After that, what he needs most is some intelligent neglect. —Ivy Baker Priest

· · · · ·

A birthday is a good time to begin anew: throwing away the old habits, as you would old clothes, and never putting them on again. —Bronson Alcott

· · · · ·

Growth is the only evidence of life. —John Henry Newman

· · · · ·

SOME PEOPLE ARE SO MUCH SUNSHINE TO THE SQUARE INCH.

—Walt Whitman

· · · · ·

The most difficult thing in the world is to know how to do a thing and to watch someone else do it wrong, without comment. —T. H. White

· · · · ·

"If everybody minded their own business," the Duchess said in a hoarse growl, "the world would go round a good deal faster than it does." —Lewis Carroll

Live a life as a monument to your soul. —Ayn Rand

. . . . .

We boil at different degrees. —Ralph Waldo Emerson

. . . . .

I would feel more optimistic about a bright future for man if
he spent less time proving that he can outwit Nature and more
time tasting her sweetness and respecting her seniority.

—E. B. White

. . . . .

Men occasionally stumble over the truth, but most of them
pick themselves up and hurry on as if nothing had happened.

—Sir Winston Churchill

. . . . .

SERVICE TO OTHERS IS THE RENT YOU PAY FOR YOUR ROOM HERE ON EARTH.

—Muhammad Ali

. . . . .

The best and safest thing is to keep a balance in your life,
acknowledge the great powers around us and in us. If you can
do that, and live that way, you are really a wise man. —Euripides

. . . . .

Life is a great big canvas; throw all the paint you can at it.

—Danny Kaye

You gain strength, courage and confidence by every experience in which you really stop to look fear in the face. You are able to say to yourself, "I lived through this horror. I can take the next thing that comes along." —Eleanor Roosevelt

Nearly all men can stand adversity, but if you want to test a man's character, give him power. —Abraham Lincoln

Know how sublime a thing is to suffer and be strong.
—Henry Wadsworth Longfellow

This above all: to thine own self be true,
And it must follow, as the night the day,
Thou canst not then be false to any man. —William Shakespeare

Education is the best provision for the journey to old age.

—Aristotle

I am never afraid of what I know. —Anna Sewell

ON THE WHOLE, HUMAN BEINGS WANT TO BE GOOD, BUT NOT TOO GOOD AND NOT QUITE ALL THE TIME.

—George Orwell

· · · · ·

He has great tranquility of heart who cares neither for the praises nor the fault-finding of men. —Honoré de Balzac

· · · · ·

The man who insists upon seeing with perfect clearness before he decides, never decides. Accept life, and you must accept regret. —Henri Frédéric Amiel

· · · · ·

The majority of men are bundles of beginnings.

—Ralph Waldo Emerson

· · · · ·

The childhood shows the man, as morning shows the day. —John Milton

· · · · ·

Life is an adventure in forgiveness.

—Norman Cousins

· · · · ·

Never be haughty to the humble; never be humble to the haughty. —Jefferson Davis

· · · · ·

There is no reason why the same man should like the same book at 18 and at 48. —Ezra Pound

The young always have the same problem—how to rebel and conform at the same time. They have solved this by defying their parents and copying one another. —Quentin Crisp

· · · · ·

If all misfortunes were laid in one common heap whence everyone must take an equal portion, most people would be contented to take their own and depart. —Socrates

· · · · ·

DON'T JUDGE EACH DAY BY THE HARVEST YOU REAP, BUT BY THE SEEDS YOU PLANT.

—Robert Louis Stevenson

· · · · ·

One reason why birds and horses are not unhappy is because they are not trying to impress other birds and horses.

—Dale Carnegie

· · · · ·

Many people genuinely do not wish to be saints, and it is possible that some who achieve or aspire to sainthood have never had much temptation to be human beings. —George Orwell

. . . . .

To say yes, you have to sweat and roll up your sleeves and plunge both hands into life up to the elbows. It's easy to say no, even if it means dying. —Jean Anouilh

. . . . .

A DEAD THING CAN GO WITH THE STREAM, BUT ONLY A LIVING THING CAN GO AGAINST IT.

—G. K. Chesterton

. . . . .

When you are younger you get blamed for crimes you never committed and when you're older you begin to get credit for virtues you never possessed. It evens itself out. —George Santayana

. . . . .

Life is an echo. What you send out—you get back. What you give—you get. —Anonymous

. . . . .

Life is like playing a violin in public and learning the instrument as one goes on. —Samuel Butler

. . . . .

Life consists not in holding good cards but in playing those you hold well. —Josh Billings

· · · · ·

If you can't make it better, you can laugh at it. —Erma Bombeck

· · · · ·

Character is much easier kept than recovered. —Thomas Paine

· · · · ·

Life is the art of drawing sufficient conclusions from insufficient premises. —Samuel Butler

· · · · ·

The future comes one day at a time. —Dean Acheson

· · · · ·

Do well and you will have no need for ancestors. —Voltaire

· · · · ·

THIS IS THE FIRST TEST OF A GENTLEMAN: HIS RESPECT FOR THOSE WHO CAN BE OF NO POSSIBLE VALUE TO HIM. —William Lyon Phelps

· · · · ·

Life Lessons
Our Top 10 Favorites

What, exactly, is the meaning of life? Some say that it's a little like cooking: sometimes you follow a recipe and sometimes you just wing it. And with each recipe (followed or winged) a lesson can be learned. Here are just a few.

Don't worry about avoiding temptation . . . as you grow older, it will avoid you.

—Winston Churchill

From what we get, we can make a living; what we give, however, makes a life. —Arthur Ashe

Nature gives you the face you have at twenty; it is up to you to merit the face you have at fifty. —Coco Chanel

Life is uncertain. Eat dessert first.

—Ernestine Ulmer

[Life] is a little like wrestling a gorilla. You don't quit when you're tired—you quit when the gorilla is tired. —Robert Strauss

A good time for laughing is when you can.

—Jessamyn West

A day without laughter is a day wasted.

—Charlie Chaplin

In three words I can sum up everything I've learned about life: It goes on.

—Robert Frost

Start every day off with a smile and get it over with. —W. C. Fields

He who has health has hope. And he who has hope has everything.

—Arabian proverb

The strongest man in the world is he who stands alone.

—Henrik Ibsen

· · · · ·

The measure of a man is the way he bears up under misfortune. —Plutarch

· · · · ·

Hope springs eternal in the human breast: / Man never is, but always to be blest. —Alexander Pope

· · · · ·

A mature person is one who does not think only in absolutes, who is able to be objective even when deeply stirred emotionally, who has learned that there is both good and bad in all people and all things, and who walks humbly and deals charitably with the circumstances of life. —Eleanor Roosevelt

· · · · ·

IT IS NOT ONLY FOR WHAT WE DO THAT WE ARE HELD RESPONSIBLE, BUT ALSO FOR WHAT WE DO NOT DO.

—Molière

· · · · ·

The older I grow the more I distrust the familiar doctrine that age brings wisdom. —H. L. Mencken

The moment we begin to fear the opinions of others and hesitate to tell the truth that is in us, and from motives of policy are silent when we should speak, the divine floods of light and life no longer flow into our souls. —Elizabeth Cady Stanton

· · · · ·

People travel to wonder at the height of the mountains, at the huge waves of the seas, at the long course of the rivers, at the vast compass of the ocean, at the circular motion of the stars, and yet they pass by themselves without wondering.

—Saint Augustine

· · · · ·

Be grateful for luck. Pay the thunder no mind—listen to the birds. And don't hate nobody. —Eubie Blake

· · · · ·

Go confidently in the direction of your dreams! Live the life you've imagined. As you simplify your life, the laws of the universe will be simpler. —Henry David Thoreau

· · · · ·

... BEFORE I CAN LIVE WITH OTHER FOLKS I'VE GOT TO LIVE WITH MYSELF. THE ONE THING THAT DOESN'T ABIDE BY MAJORITY RULE IS A PERSON'S CONSCIENCE. —Harper Lee

· · · · ·

Never feel self-pity, the most destructive emotion there is.
How awful to be caught up in the terrible squirrel cage of self.
—Millicent Fenwick

· · · · ·

If you cry because the sun has gone out of your life, your tears
will prevent you from seeing the stars. — Rabindranath Tagore

· · · · ·

Time is the wisest counselor. —Pericles

· · · · ·

A man's heart away from nature becomes hard; lack of
respect for growing, living things soon leads to a lack of
respect for humans too. —Luther Standing Bear

· · · · ·

Happiness is always a by-product. It is probably a matter of
temperament, and for anything I know it may be glandular.
But it is not something that can be demanded from life, and if
you are not happy you had better stop worrying about it.
—Robertson Davies

Live your questions now, and perhaps even without knowing it, you will live along some distant day into your answers.

—Rainer Maria Rilke

· · · · · ·

May you have a strong foundation when the winds of changes shift . . . and may you be forever young. —Bob Dylan

· · · · · ·

Do not go where the path may lead, go instead where there is no path and leave a trail. —Ralph Waldo Emerson

· · · · · ·

The mass of men lead lives of quiet desperation.

—Henry David Thoreau

· · · · · ·

To succeed in life, you need two things: ignorance and confidence. —Mark Twain

· · · · · ·

Never let yesterday use up too much of today.
—Will Rogers

Reflect upon your present blessings, of which every man has plenty; not on your past misfortunes of which all men have some. —Charles Dickens

· · · · · ·

I can resist everything except temptation. —Oscar Wilde

. . . . . .

Expect nothing. Live frugally on surprise. —Alice Walker

. . . . . .

A great secret of success is to go through life as a man who never gets used up. —Albert Schweitzer

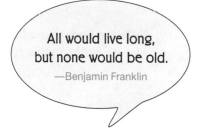

All would live long, but none would be old.
—Benjamin Franklin

. . . . . .

Just trust yourself, then you will know how to live.

—Johann Wolfgang von Goethe

. . . . . .

A man of good will with a little effort and belief in his own powers can enjoy a deep, tranquil, rich life—provided he go his own way. . . . To live one's own life is still the best way of life, always was, and always will be. —Henry Miller

. . . . . .

If only I may grow: firmer, simpler—quieter, warmer.

—Dag Hammarskjöld

. . . . . .

This existence of ours is as transient as autumn clouds. To watch the birth and death of beings is like looking at the movements of a dance. A lifetime is a flash of lightning in the sky. Rushing by, like a torrent down a steep mountain.

—Buddha

· · · · ·

We are here to laugh at the odds and live our lives so well that Death will tremble to take us. —Charles Bukowski

· · · · ·

Death is nothing to us, since when we are, death has not come, and when death has come, we are not. —Epicurus

· · · · ·

We are no more than candles burning in the wind.

—Japanese proverb

· · · · ·

Live so that you wouldn't be ashamed to sell the family parrot to the town gossip. —Will Rogers

· · · · ·

YOU ARE NEVER TOO OLD TO BE WHAT YOU MIGHT HAVE BEEN.

—George Eliot

· · · · ·

It is in self-limitation that a master first shows himself.

—Johann Wolfgang von Goethe

. . . . .

In the long run, we shape our lives, and we shape ourselves. The process never ends until we die. And the choices we make are ultimately our own responsibility. —Eleanor Roosevelt

. . . . .

The mere process of growing old together will make the slightest acquaintance seem a bosom friend.

—Logan Pearsall Smith

. . . . .

IF I KNEW I WAS GOING TO LIVE THIS LONG, I'D HAVE TAKEN BETTER CARE OF MYSELF.
—Mickey Mantle *Satchel Paige*

. . . . .

I went to the woods because I wished to live deliberately, to front only the essential facts of life and see if I could not learn what they had to teach; and not, when I came to die, discover that I had not lived. —Henry David Thoreau, *Walden*

. . . . .

People—some good, some bad, but in the long run we come out even. —Jan Hittle

As a well-spent day brings happy sleep, so a life well spent brings happy death. —Leonardo da Vinci

· · · · ·

IN AN ARTIST'S LIFE, DEATH IS PERHAPS NOT THE MOST DIFFICULT THING.

—Vincent van Gogh

· · · · ·

Death—the last sleep? No, it is the final awakening.

—Sir Walter Scott

· · · · ·

Lord, how the day passes! It's like a life—so quickly when we don't watch it and so slowly if we do. —John Steinbeck

· · · · ·

Hope is a good breakfast, but it is a bad supper.

—Sir Francis Bacon

I have discovered that all human evil comes from this: man's being unable to sit still and quiet in a room alone.

—Blaise Pascal

· · · · ·

It is said an Eastern monarch once charged his wise men to invent him a sentence, to be ever in view, and which should be true and appropriate in all times and situations. They presented him the words: And this, too, shall pass away.

—Abraham Lincoln

No man is an Island, entire of itself; every man is a piece of the Continent, a part of the main; if a clod be washed away by the sea, Europe is the less, as well as if a promontory were, as well as if a manor of thy friends or of thine own were; any man's death diminishes me, because I am involved in Mankind; And therefore never send to know for whom the bell tolls; It tolls for thee.

—John Donne

I want to live my life so that my nights are not full of regrets.

—D. H. Lawrence

I promise to keep on living as though I expected to live forever. Nobody grows old by merely living a number of years. People grow old by deserting their ideals. Years may wrinkle the skin, but to give up wrinkles the soul.

—Douglas MacArthur

May you live all the days of your life. —Jonathan Swift

Live simply, that others may simply live. —Mohandas Gandhi

Let us not look back in anger, nor forward in fear, but around in awareness. —James Thurber

· · · · ·

My advice to you is not to inquire why or whither, but just enjoy your ice cream while it's on your plate—that's my philosophy. —Thornton Wilder

· · · · ·

Enjoy the spring of love and youth,
To some good angel leave the rest;
For time will teach thee soon the truth,
There are no birds in last year's nest.

—Henry Wadsworth Longfellow

> Old age ain't no place for sissies.
> —Bette Davis

· · · · ·

Experience is a hard teacher. She gives the test first and the lessons afterwards. —Anonymous

· · · · ·

Know the true value of time; snatch, seize, and enjoy every moment of it. No idleness, no laziness, no procrastination: never put off till to-morrow what you can do to-day.

—Philip Dormer Stanhope, Lord Chesterfield

· · · · ·

No man is rich enough to buy back his past. —Oscar Wilde

· ·

32

Live as long as you can. Die when you can't help it. —James Brown

· · · · ·

In times like these, it helps to recall that there have always been times like these. —Paul Harvey

· · · · ·

Make voyages! Attempt them . . . there's nothing else.

—Tennessee Williams

· · · · ·

The best portion of a good man's life is his little, nameless, unremembered acts of kindness and of love. —William Wordsworth

· · · · ·

THE YEARS BETWEEN FIFTY AND SEVENTY ARE THE HARDEST. YOU ARE ALWAYS BEING ASKED TO DO THINGS, AND YET YOU ARE NOT DECREPIT ENOUGH TO TURN THEM DOWN.

—T. S. Eliot

· · · · ·

Grow old along with me! / The best is yet to be. —Robert Browning

· · · · ·

· ·

33

The only man who behaves sensibly is my tailor; he takes my measure anew every time he sees me, whilst all the rest go on with their old measurements, and expect them to fit me.

—George Bernard Shaw

· · · · ·

One of the secrets of a long and fruitful life is to forgive everybody everything every night before you go to bed.

—Bernard Mannes Baruch

· · · · ·

Don't look back. Something might be gaining on you.

—Satchel Paige

· · · · ·

The greatest thing in life is to die young—but delay it as long as possible.
—George Bernard Shaw

Don't hurry, don't worry. You're here for a short visit. So be sure to stop and smell the flowers. —Walter Hagen

· · · · ·

Millions long for immortality who do not know what to do with themselves on a rainy Sunday afternoon. —Susan Ertz

· · · · ·

Old age is like everything else. To make a success of it, you've got to start young. —Fred Astaire

· · · · ·

Since time is not a person we can overtake when he is past, let us honor him with mirth and cheerfulness of heart while he is passing. —Johann Wolfgang von Goethe

· · · · ·

To be idle is a short road to death and to be diligent is a way of life; foolish people are idle, wise people are diligent. —Buddha

I HAVE AN IRREPRESSIBLE DESIRE TO LIVE TILL I CAN BE ASSURED THAT THE WORLD IS A LITTLE BETTER FOR MY HAVING LIVED IN IT.

—Abraham Lincoln

· · · · ·

Man is the only animal that blushes. Or needs to. —Mark Twain

· · · · ·

The tragedy of life is not so much what men suffer, but rather what they miss. —Thomas Carlyle

· · · · ·

I like living. I have sometimes been wildly, despairingly, acutely miserable, racked with sorrow, but through it all I still know quite certainly that just to be alive is a grand thing.

—Agatha Christie

· · · · ·

Taking joy in life is a woman's best cosmetic. —Rosalind Russell

• • • • •

Judge a man by his questions rather than his answers. —Voltaire

• • • • •

The greatest pleasure in life is doing what people say you cannot do. —Walter Bagehot

• • • • •

The difference between life and the movies is that a script has to make sense, and life doesn't. —Joseph L. Mankiewicz

Never, never rest contented with any circle of ideas, but always be certain that a wider one is still possible. —Pearl Bailey

• • • • •

It is hard to have patience with people who say There is no death or Death doesn't matter. There is death. And whatever is matters. And whatever happens has consequences, and it and they are irrevocable and irreversible. You might as well say that birth doesn't matter. —C. S. Lewis

• • • • •

Good advice is something a man gives when he is too old to set a bad example. —François de La Rochefoucauld

· · · · ·

THE BITTEREST TEARS SHED OVER GRAVES ARE FOR WORDS LEFT UNSAID AND DEEDS LEFT UNDONE.

—Harriet Beecher Stowe

· · · · ·

There is, therefore, only one categorical imperative. It is: Act only according to that maxim by which you can at the same time will that it should become a universal law. —Immanuel Kant

· · · · ·

How wonderful it is that nobody need wait a single moment before starting to improve the world. —Anne Frank

· · · · ·

What the superior man seeks is in himself. What the mean man seeks is in others. —Confucius

· · · · ·

COURAGE IS CONTAGIOUS. WHEN A BRAVE MAN TAKES A STAND, THE SPINES OF OTHERS ARE STIFFENED.

—Billy Graham

Lying to ourselves is more deeply ingrained than lying to others. —Fyodor Mikhaylovich Dostoyevsky

· · · · ·

Cowards die many times before their deaths; The valiant never taste death but once. —William Shakespeare

· · · · ·

HATEFUL TO ME AS THE GATES OF HADES IS THAT MAN WHO HIDES ONE THING IN HIS HEART AND SPEAKS ANOTHER.

—Homer

· · · · ·

Your vision will become clear only when you can look into your own heart. Who looks outside, dreams; who looks inside, awakens. —Carl Jung

It is a human nature to think wisely and act foolishly.

—Anatole France

· · · · ·

Everything should be as simple as it is, but not simpler.

—Albert Einstein

· · · · ·

You Can't Take it With You
10 Wise Tidbits On The Grim Reaper

Try a cure, lose weight, gain weight, eat healthy, or eat badly . . . we'll do anything to keep the robed skeleton from paying a visit.

Never go to a doctor whose office plants have died. —Erma Bombeck

There's nothing wrong with you that reincarnation won't cure.

—Jack E. Leonard

Don't worry about the world coming to an end today. It's already tomorrow in Australia.

—Charles Schultz

Die a beggar.

—Antony & Cleopatra

Be careful about reading health books. You may die of a misprint.

—Mark Twain

Do not try to live forever. You will not succeed.

—George Bernard Shaw

It is not what we do, but also what we do not do, for which we are accountable.

—Jean Baptiste Molière

Dying is a very dull, dreary affair. And my advice to you is to have nothing whatever to do with it. —W. Somerset Maugham

Death is not the greatest loss in life. The greatest loss is what dies inside us while we live. —Norman Cousins

I pray a thousand prayers for thy death; no words to save thee.

—Measure for Measure

A man has to live with himself, and he should see to it that he always has good company. —Charles Evans Hughes

· · · · ·

If you enjoy living, it is not difficult to keep the sense of wonder. —Ray Bradbury

· · · · ·

Wrinkles should merely indicate where smiles have been.
—Mark Twain

Worry is like a rocking chair, it will give you something to do, but it won't get you anywhere. —Anonymous

· · · · ·

Silence is argument carried on by other means.

—Ernesto "Che" Guevara

· · · · ·

The gentle mind by gentle deeds is known. For a man by nothing is so well betrayed, as by his manners. —Edmund Spenser

· · · · ·

Let us then suppose the mind to be, as we say, a white paper, void of all characters, without any ideas. How comes it to be furnished? . . . To this I answer, in one word, from experience.

—John Locke

· · · · ·

Believe not because some old manuscripts are produced, believe not because it is your national belief, believe not because you have been made to believe from your childhood, but reason truth out, and after you have analyzed it, then if you find it will do good to one and all, believe it, live up to it and help others live up to it. —Buddha

• • • • •

He who angers you conquers you. —Elizabeth Kenny

• • • • •

EVERYONE CAN MASTER A GRIEF BUT HE THAT HAS IT.

—William Shakespeare

• • • • •

As blushing will sometimes make a whore pass for a virtuous woman, so modesty may make a fool seem a man of sense.

—Jonathan Swift

• • • • •

Sooner or later we all discover that the important moments in life are not the advertised ones, not the birthdays, the graduations, the weddings, not the great goals achieved. The real milestones are less prepossessing. They come to the door of memory unannounced, stray dogs that amble in, sniff around a bit and simply never leave. Our lives are measured by these. —Susan B. Anthony

• • • • •

Without music, life is a journey through a desert. —Pat Conroy

· · · · ·

Use your health, even to the point of wearing it out. That is what it is for. Spend all you have before you die; and do not outlive yourself. —George Bernard Shaw

· · · · ·

For of all sad words of tongue or pen / the saddest are these; It might have been! —John Greenleaf Whittier

· · · · ·

A thing is not necessarily true because a man dies for it.

—Oscar Wilde

· · · · ·

GROWING OLD IS NO MORE THAN A BAD HABIT THAT A BUSY PERSON HAS NOT TIME TO FORM.

—André Maurois

· · · · ·

If you think about disaster, you will get it. Brood about death and you hasten your demise. Think positively and masterfully, with confidence and faith, and life becomes more secure, more fraught with action, richer in achievement and experience. —Swami Sivananda

· · · · ·

The act of dying is also one of the acts of life. —Marcus Aurelius

· · · · ·

Old age is far more than white hair, wrinkles, the feeling that it is too late and the game finished, that the stage belongs to the rising generations. The true evil is not the weakening of the body, but the indifference of the soul. —André Maurois

· · · · ·

A LIFETIME OF HAPPINESS! NO MAN ALIVE COULD BEAR IT: IT WOULD BE HELL ON EARTH.

—George Bernard Shaw

· · · · ·

When you're young and you fall off a horse, you may break something. When you're my age and you fall off, you splatter.

—Roy Rogers

· · · · ·

Old minds are like old horses; you must exercise them if you wish to keep them in working order. —John Adams

· · · · ·

Anyone who keeps the ability to see beauty in every age of life really never grows old. —Franz Kafka

· · · · ·

I wasted time, and now doth time waste me. —William Shakespeare

· · · · ·

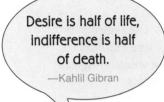

Desire is half of life,
indifference is half
of death.
—Kahlil Gibran

We can easily forgive a child who is
afraid of the dark. The real tragedy of
life is when men are afraid of the light.

—Plato

· · · · ·

And we should consider every day lost on which we have not
danced at least once. And we should call every truth false
which was not accompanied by at least one laugh.

—Friedrich Wilhelm Nietzsche

· · · · ·

WE DON'T SEE THINGS AS THEY ARE, WE SEE THEM AS WE ARE.

—Anaïs Nin

· · · · ·

The happy man is not he who seems thus to others, but who
seems thus to himself. —Marcel Proust

· · · · ·

Three o'clock is always too late or too early for anything you
want to do. —Jean-Paul Sartre

· · · · ·

No matter how dark things seem to be or actually are, raise your sights and see the possibilities—always see them, for they're always there. —Norman Vincent Peale

· · · · ·

In order for three people to keep a secret, two must be dead.

—Benjamin Franklin

· · · · ·

My hopes are not always realized, but I always hope. —Ovid

· · · · ·

Sometimes a cigar is just a cigar. —Sigmund Freud

· · · · ·

All is for the best in the best of all possible worlds. —Voltaire

If man hasn't discovered something that he will die for, he isn't fit to live.
—Martin Luther King, Jr.

· · · · ·

Whatever befalls the earth befalls the sons and daughters of the earth. We did not weave the web of life; We are merely a strand in it. What we do with the web, we do to ourselves . . .

—Chief Seattle

· · · · ·

The world is full of magical things patiently waiting for our wits to grow sharper. —Bertrand Russell

. . . . .

Life is pleasant. Death is peaceful. It's the transition that's troublesome. —Isaac Asimov

. . . . .

A ship ought not to be held by one anchor, nor life by a single hope. —Epictetus

. . . . .

Fear not for the future, weep not for the past.
—Percy Bysshe Shelley

. . . . .

I keep my ideals, because in spite of everything I still believe that people are really good at heart. —Anne Frank

. . . . .

I SPEAK TRUTH, NOT SO MUCH AS I WOULD, BUT AS MUCH AS I DARE; AND I DARE A LITTLE MORE, AS I GROW OLDER.

—Catherine Drinker Bowen

. . . . .

· ·

46

Sometimes our light goes out but is blown into flame by another human being. Each of us owes deepest thanks to those who have rekindled this light. —Albert Schweitzer

· · · · ·

LIFE DOES NOT CEASE TO BE FUNNY WHEN PEOPLE DIE ANY MORE THAN IT CEASES TO BE SERIOUS WHEN PEOPLE LAUGH.

—Antoine de Saint-Exupéry

· · · · ·

The great consolation in life is to say what one thinks. —Voltaire

· · · · ·

The best remedy for anger is delay. —Brigham Young

· · · · ·

Sweet is a grief well ended. —Aeschylus

· · · · ·

Men fear death, as children fear to go in the dark; and as that natural fear in children is increased with tales, so is the other.

—Sir Francis Bacon

· · · · ·

Be of good cheer about death and know this as a truth—that no evil can happen to a good man, either in life or after death.

—Socrates

· · · · ·

Our fear of death is like our fear that summer will be short, but when we have had our swing of pleasure, our fill of fruit, and our swelter of heat, we say we have had our day.

—Ralph Waldo Emerson

· · · · ·

The longer I live, the more beautiful life becomes.

—Frank Lloyd Wright

· · · · ·

It's not over until it's over. —Yogi Berra

· · · · ·

DEATH ENDS A LIFE, NOT A RELATIONSHIP.

—Jack Lemmon

· · · · ·

NEITHER FIRE NOR WIND, BIRTH NOR DEATH CAN ERASE OUR GOOD DEEDS.

—Buddha

· · · · ·

When I look back on all these worries, I remember the story of the old man who said on his deathbed that he had had a lot of trouble in his life, most of which had never happened.

—Sir Winston Churchill

· · · · ·

How far you go in life depends on your being tender with the young, compassionate with the aged, sympathetic with the striving, and tolerant of the weak and strong. Because someday in your life you will have been all of these.

—George Washington Carver

· · · · ·

I always remember an epitaph which is in the cemetery at Tombstone, Arizona. It says: "Here lies Jack Williams. He done his damnedest." I think that is the greatest epitaph a man can have. —Harry S Truman

· · · · ·

In the end, everything is a gag. —Charlie Chaplin

· · · · ·

What is a friend? A single soul dwelling in two bodies.

—Aristotle

Chapter 2

Love and Friendship

*L*ove *(usually) starts with friendship, with a kind word, a sidelong glance—hearts pound, butterflies flutter—and so it begins. Take a glance at these wise words and feel the beauty of the thing that makes life so wonderful.*

And in the end, the love you take is equal to the love you make.
—Paul McCartney

. . . . .

Always be a little kinder than necessary.
—Sir James Matthew Barrie

. . . . .

People are unreasonable, illogical, and self-centered. Love them anyway. —Mother Teresa

. . . . .

TO ERR IS HUMAN, TO FORGIVE DIVINE.
—Alexander Pope

To err is human; to forgive, infrequent. —Franklin P. Adams

· · · · ·

A person is only as good as what they love. —Saul Bellow

· · · · ·

To give counsel as well as to take it is a feature of true friendship. —Marcus Tullius Cicero

· · · · ·

THOUSANDS OF CANDLES CAN BE LIGHTED FROM A SINGLE CANDLE, AND THE LIFE OF THE CANDLE WILL NOT BE SHORTENED. HAPPINESS NEVER DECREASES BY BEING SHARED.

—Buddha

· · · · ·

Kind hearts are more than coronets / And simple faith than Norman blood. —Alfred, Lord Tennyson

· · · · ·

A heart can be broken, but it will keep beating just the same.
—Fannie Flagg

· · · · ·

Love is like war; easy to begin but very hard to stop.

—H. L. Mencken

· · · · ·

Though you break your heart, men will go on as before.

—Marcus Aurelius

· · · · ·

It is well, when judging a friend, to remember that he is judging you with the same godlike and superior impartiality. —Arnold Bennett

Have a heart that never hardens, a temper that never tires, a touch that never hurts.

—Charles Dickens

· · · · ·

I count myself in nothing else so happy / As in a soul rememb'ring my good friends. —William Shakespeare

· · · · ·

The heart has its reasons of which reason knows nothing.

—Blaise Pascal

· · · · ·

Few men have the natural strength to honour a friend's success without envy. —Aeschylus

· · · · ·

To give pleasure to a single heart by a single kind act is better than a thousand head-bowings in prayer. —Saadi

• • • • •

Goodness does not consist in greatness, but greatness in goodness. —Athenaeus

• • • • •

LOVE IS A GREAT BEAUTIFIER.
—Louisa May Alcott

• • • • •

If you have only one smile in you, give it to the people you love. Don't be surly at home, then go out in the street and start grinning "Good morning" at total strangers. —Maya Angelou

• • • • •

There might be some credit in being jolly. —Charles Dickens

• • • • •

Without friends no one would choose to live, though he had all other goods. —Aristotle

• • • • •

An insincere and evil friend is more to be feared than a wild beast; a wild beast may wound your body, but an evil friend will wound your mind. —Buddha

Love Lessons

10 Tasty Quotes on Amour

Love got you down? No need for counseling, you're not going crazy—and put down the chocolate bar! There's no right or wrong way to be in love; it's not logical . . . it's pure emotion!

A loving heart is the truest wisdom.
—Charles Dickens

Laughter is the closest distance between two people. —Victor Borge

Spread love everywhere you go. Let no one ever come to you without leaving happier.
—Mother Teresa

The best proof of love is trust.
—Dr. Joyce Brothers

When you fish for love, bait with your heart, not your brain. —Mark Twain

Love is everything it's cracked up to be . . . It really is worth fighting for, being brave for, risking everything for. —Erica Jong

Do not walk behind me; I may not lead. Do not walk in front of me; I may not follow. Walk beside me, that we may be as one. —Ute saying

Love is an irresistible desire to be irresistably desired. —Robert Frost

If you wish to be loved, show more of your faults than your virtues.
—Edward Bulwer-Lytton

There is no remedy for love but to love more.
—Henry David Thoreau

It is a good thing to be rich and a good thing to be strong, but it is a better thing to be loved by many friends. —Euripides

. . . . . .

IT'S SAD WHEN SOMEONE YOU KNOW
BECOMES SOMEONE YOU KNEW.

—Henry Rollins

. . . . . .

Your friends will know you better in the first moment you meet than your acquaintances will know you in a lifetime.

—Richard Bach

. . . . . .

It is in pardoning that we are pardoned. —Saint Francis of Assisi

. . . . . .

In those whom I like, I can find no common denominator; in those whom I love I can: they all make me laugh. —W. H. Auden

. . . . . .

Those who bring sunshine to the lives of others cannot keep it from themselves. —Sir James Matthew Barrie

. . . . . .

Friendship is like money, easier made than kept. —Samuel Butler

One of the surest evidences of friendship that one individual can display to another is telling him gently of a fault. If any other can excel it, it is listening to such a disclosure with gratitude, and amending the error. —Edward Bulwer-Lytton

I always felt that the great high privilege, relief and comfort of friendship was that one had to explain nothing.

—Katherine Mansfield

If you want to win friends, make it a point to remember them. If you remember my name, you pay me a subtle compliment; you indicate that I have made an impression on you. Remember my name and you add to my feeling of importance. —Dale Carnegie

If you would stand well with a great mind, leave him with a favorable impression of yourself; if with a little mind, leave him with a favorable impression of himself.

—Samuel Taylor Coleridge

You shall judge a man by his foes as well as by his friends.

—Joseph Conrad

As old wood is best to burn; old horses to ride; old books to read; old wine to drink; so are old friends most trusty to use.

—Leonard Wright

· · · · ·

A friend is a person with whom I may be sincere. Before him, I may think aloud. —Ralph Waldo Emerson

· · · · ·

A loving heart is the truest wisdom. —Charles Dickens

· · · · ·

WE MUST DEVELOP AND MAINTAIN THE CAPACITY TO FORGIVE. HE WHO IS DEVOID OF THE POWER TO FORGIVE IS DEVOID OF THE POWER TO LOVE. THERE IS SOME GOOD IN THE WORST OF US AND SOME EVIL IN THE BEST OF US.

—Martin Luther King, Jr.

· · · · ·

A true friend is the greatest of all blessings, and that which we take the least care of all to acquire.

—François de La Rochefoucauld

· · · · ·

How should we like it / were stars to burn / With a passion for us we / could not return / If equal affection there cannot be / Let the more loving one be me. —W. H. Auden

· · · · ·

Friendship is born at that moment when one person says to another: What! You, too? I thought I was the only one.

—C. S. Lewis

· · · · ·

The glory of friendship is not the outstretched hand, nor the kindly smile, nor the joy of companionship; it is the spiritual inspiration that comes to one when you discover that someone else believes in you and is willing to trust you with a friendship. —Ralph Waldo Emerson

· · · · ·

Love is a canvas furnished by Nature and embroidered by imagination. —Voltaire

· · · · ·

THE MOST I CAN DO FOR MY FRIEND IS SIMPLY TO BE HIS FRIEND.

—Henry David Thoreau

· · · · ·

"Hey there, big boy. . . . ."
The Beginnings of a Love Story? (Anything's possible.)

Man: May I see you pretty soon?

Woman: Why? Don't you think I'm pretty now?

Man: I'd go through anything for you.

Woman: Good! Let's start with your bank account.

Man: Can I buy you a drink?

Woman: Actually I'd rather have the money.

Man: Your face must turn a few heads.

Woman: And your face must turn a few stomachs.

Man: How did you get to be so beautiful?

Woman: I must've been given your share.

Man: Can I have your name!

Woman: Why? Don't you already have one?

Man: Hi. Didn't we go on a date once? Or was it twice?

Woman: Must've been once. I never make the same mistake twice.

Man: Where have you been all my life?

Woman: Where I'll be the rest of your life—in your wildest dreams.

Man: What would you say if I asked you to marry me?

Woman: Nothing. I can't talk and laugh at the same time.

Man: Go on, don't be shy. Ask me out.

Woman: Okay, get out.

If I can stop one heart from breaking, If I can ease one pain, /
Then my life will not have been in vain. —Emily Elizabeth Dickinson

• • • • •

Ah, when to the heart of man / Was it ever less than a treason
/ To go with the drift of things / To yield with a grace to reason
/ And bow and accept at the end / Of a love or a season.

—Robert Frost

• • • • •

Listening is a magnetic and strange thing, a creative force.
The friends who listen to us are the ones we move toward.
When we are listened to, it creates us, makes us unfold and
expand. —Dr. Karl Augustus Menninger

I have learned that to be with those I like is enough.

—Walt Whitman

• • • • •

HOLD A TRUE FRIEND WITH BOTH YOUR HANDS.
—Friedrich Wilhelm Nietzsche

• • • • •

Absence is to love what wind is to fire; it extinguishes the
small, it enkindles the great. —Comte Roger de Bussy-Rabutin

• • • • •

A kiss is a rosy dot over the "i" of loving. —Cyrano de Bergerac

· · · · ·

My friend is one who takes me for what I am.

—Henry David Thoreau

· · · · ·

IMMATURE LOVE SAYS: "I LOVE YOU BECAUSE I NEED YOU." MATURE LOVE SAYS "I NEED YOU BECAUSE I LOVE YOU."

—Erich Fromm

· · · · ·

True friendship is like sound health; the value of it is seldom known until it be lost. —Charles Caleb Colton

· · · · ·

A real friend is one who walks in when the rest of the world walks out. —Anonymous

· · · · ·

A friend is a present you give yourself.
—Robert Louis Stevenson

Kindness is more important than wisdom, and the recognition of this is the beginning of wisdom. —Theodore Isaac Rubin

· · · · ·

Forget injuries, never forget kindnesses. —Confucius

. . . . . .

Familiar acts are beautiful through love. —Percy Bysshe Shelley

. . . . . .

A friend is someone who can sing you the song of your heart when you've forgotten it. —Anonymous

. . . . . .

The greatest good you can do for another is not just to share your riches but to reveal to him his own. —Benjamin Disraeli

. . . . . .

Tis better to have loved and lost / Than never to have loved at all. —Alfred, Lord Tennyson

. . . . . .

We cannot all do great things, but we can do small things with great love. —Mother Teresa

. . . . . .

To love and win is the best thing. To love and lose, the next best. —William Makepeace Thackeray

. . . . . .

The indispensable first step to getting the things you want out of life is this: Decide what you want.

—Ben Stein

Chapter 3

A Bright Endeavor

How do you measure success? With the amassing of money, the number of toys, the luxuriant lifestyle? Make no mistake. Those things are quite nice, but they're not everything. Ponder these sage words and imagine the possibilities.

Success is the ability to go from one failure to another with no loss of enthusiasm. —Sir Winston Churchill

. . . . .

THE OBSTACLE IS THE PATH. —Zen aphorism

. . . . .

You have brains in your head
You have feet in your shoes
You can steer yourself
any direction you choose
You're on your own. And you know what you know.
And YOU are the guy who'll decide where to go.

—Dr. Seuss (Theodore Geisel)

Genius is one percent inspiration and ninety-nine percent perspiration. —Thomas Alva Edison

· · · · ·

It is not enough to be busy. . . . The question is: what are we busy about? —Henry David Thoreau

· · · · ·

All good things which exist are the fruits of originality.

—John Stuart Mill

· · · · ·

The future belongs to those who believe in the beauty of their dreams.
—Eleanor Roosevelt

The person who makes a success of living is the one who sees his goal steadily and aims for it unswervingly.

—Cecil B. DeMille

· · · · ·

Things turn out best for the people who make the best of the way things turn out. —John R. Wooden

· · · · ·

IN THE FIELD OF OBSERVATION, CHANCE FAVORS THE PREPARED MIND.

—Louis Pasteur

· · · · ·

The best way to make your dreams come true is to wake up.

—Paul Valéry

* * * * *

Any activity becomes creative when the doer cares about doing it right, or better. —John Updike

* * * * *

Be wiser than other people, if you can; but do not tell them so.

—Philip Dormer Stanhope, Lord Chesterfield

* * * * *

NO ILLUSION IS MORE CRUCIAL THAN THE ILLUSION THAT GREAT SUCCESS AND HUGE MONEY BUY YOU IMMUNITY FROM THE COMMON ILLS OF MANKIND, SUCH AS CARS THAT WON'T START.

—Larry McMurtry

* * * * *

There is only one boss: the customer. And he can fire everybody in the company, from the chairman on down, simply by spending his money somewhere else. —Sam Walton

* * * * *

Take calculated risks. That is quite different from being rash.

—George Smith Patton, Jr.

If it be now, 'tis not to come; if it be not to come, it will be now; if it be not now, yet it will come: the readiness is all.

—William Shakespeare

· · · · ·

The secret of successful managing is to keep the five guys who hate you away from the four guys who haven't made up their minds. —Charles "Casey" Stengel

· · · · ·

IN READING THE LIVES OF GREAT MEN, I FOUND THAT THE FIRST VICTORY THEY WON WAS OVER THEMSELVES . . . SELF-DISCIPLINE WITH ALL OF THEM CAME FIRST.

—Harry S Truman

· · · · ·

Never think that you're not good enough yourself. A man should never think that. People will take you very much at your own reckoning. —Anthony Trollope

· · · · ·

It is necessary for us to learn from others' mistakes. You will not live long enough to make them all yourself.

—Hyman George Rickover

· · · · ·

A wise man sees as much as he ought, not as much as he can.

—Michel de Montaigne

· · · · ·

Without leaps of imagination, or dreaming, we lose the excitement of possibilities. Dreaming, after all, is a form of planning. —Gloria Steinem

· · · · ·

The man who trims himself to suit everybody will soon whittle himself away. —Charles Schwab

· · · · ·

Some people believe that holding on and hanging in there are signs of great strength. However, there are times when it takes much more strength to know when to let go—and then do it.

—Ann Landers

· · · · ·

The greater danger for most of us lies not in setting our aim too high and falling short, but in setting our aim too low, and achieving our mark. —Michelangelo

· · · · ·

The cure for boredom is curiosity. There is no cure for curiosity.

—Ellen Parr

With self-discipline most anything is possible.

—Theodore Roosevelt

I don't know the key to success, but the key to failure is trying to please everybody. —Bill Cosby

· · · · ·

I always tried to turn every disaster into an opportunity.

—John D. Rockefeller, Jr.

For most of history, Anonymous was a woman.

—Virginia Woolf

· · · · ·

Fortune favors the brave. —Terence

· · · · ·

I'm a great believer in luck, and I find the harder I work the more I have of it. —Thomas Jefferson

· · · · ·

ONE OF THE ADVANTAGES OF BEING DISORDERLY IS THAT ONE IS CONSTANTLY MAKING EXCITING DISCOVERIES.

—A. A. Milne

· · · · ·

The bravest are surely those who have the clearest vision of what is before them, glory and danger alike, and yet notwithstanding go out to meet it. —Thucydides

· · · · ·

There is hardly anything in the world that some man can't make a little worse and sell a little cheaper, and the people who consider price only are this man's lawful prey.

—John Ruskin

· · · · ·

Oh, the tangled webs we weave / When we practice to deceive.

—Sir Walter Scott

· · · · ·

What lies behind us and what lies before us are tiny matters compared to what lies within us. —Ralph Waldo Emerson

Nothing is a waste of time if you use the experience wisely.

—Auguste Rodin

· · · · ·

NEVER LET YOUR HEAD HANG DOWN. NEVER GIVE UP AND SIT DOWN AND GRIEVE. FIND ANOTHER WAY. AND DON'T PRAY WHEN IT RAINS IF YOU DON'T PRAY WHEN THE SUN SHINES.

—Satchel Paige

· · · · ·

Work expands to fill the time available for its completion.

—Cyril Northcote Parkinson (known as Parkinson's Law)

• • • • •

If anything can go wrong, it will. —Murphy's Law (named after Air Force Captain Edward A. Murphy, an engineer working on a project to see how much sudden deceleration a human can stand in a crash)

• • • • •

I have not failed. I've just found 10,000 ways that won't work.

—Thomas Alva Edison

• • • • •

Formula for success: Underpromise and overdeliver.

—Thomas Peters

• • • • •

The best way to escape from a problem is to solve it.

—Anonymous

• • • • •

A CREATIVE MAN IS MOTIVATED BY THE DESIRE TO ACHIEVE, NOT BY THE DESIRE TO BEAT OTHERS.

—Ayn Rand

• • • • •

Know from whence you came. If you know whence you came, there are absolutely no limitations to where you can go.

—James Baldwin

· · · · · ·

Nothing succeeds like success. —Alexander Dumas

· · · · · ·

The spirit, the will to win, and the will to excel are the things that endure. These qualities are so much more important than the events that occur.

—Vince Lombardi

· · · · · ·

What is harder than rock, or softer than water? Yet soft water hollows out hard rock. Persevere. —Ovid

· · · · · ·

Prosperity is a great teacher; adversity a greater. —William Hazlitt

· · · · · ·

If I have seen further than others, it is by standing upon the shoulders of giants. —Sir Isaac Newton

· · · · · ·

PERFECTION IS ACHIEVED, NOT WHEN THERE IS NOTHING LEFT TO ADD, BUT WHEN THERE IS NOTHING LEFT TO TAKE AWAY.

—Antoine de Saint-Exupéry

· · · · ·

One of the lessons of history is that nothing is often a good thing to do and always a clever thing to say. —Will Durant

· · · · ·

It takes less time to do a thing right, than it does to explain why you did it wrong. —Henry Wadsworth Longfellow

· · · · ·

No one ever gets far unless he accomplishes the impossible at least once a day. —L. Ron Hubbard

· · · · ·

It is true greatness to have in one the frailty of a man and the security of a god. —Lucius Annaeus Seneca

· · · · ·

SUCCESS IS HOW HIGH YOU BOUNCE WHEN YOU HIT BOTTOM.

—George Smith Patton, Jr.

· · · · ·

The Rules of Success

Achieving success entails far more than being in the right place at the right time. Here are our favorite suggestions for getting ahead.

When a thing is done, it's done. Don't look back. Look forward to your next objective. —George C. Marshall

If you're walking down the right path and you're willing to keep walking, eventually you'll make progress. —President Barack Obama

The secret of business is to know something nobody else knows. —Aristotle Onassis

Don't find fault. Find a remedy. —Henry Ford

As long as you're going to be thinking anyway, think big. —Donald Trump

The secret of getting ahead is getting started. —Sally Berger

Many of life's failures are people who did not realize how close they were to success when they gave up. —Thomas A. Edison

Keep away from people who try to belittle your ambitions. Small people always do that, but the really great make you feel that you, too, can become great. —Mark Twain

Six essential qualities that are the key to success: Sincerity, personal integrity, humility, courtesy, wisdom, charity. —William Menninger

Eighty percent of success is just showing up. —Woody Allen

A BANK IS A PLACE WHERE THEY LEND YOU AN UMBRELLA IN FAIR WEATHER AND ASK FOR IT BACK WHEN IT BEGINS TO RAIN.

—Robert Frost

· · · · ·

Whether you think you can or whether you think you can't, you're right.
—Henry Ford

We often discover what will do, by finding out what will not do; and probably he who never made a mistake never made a discovery. —Samuel Smiles

· · · · ·

One thing life taught me: if you are interested, you never have to look for new interests. They come to you. When you are genuinely interested in one thing, it will always lead to something else. —Eleanor Roosevelt

· · · · ·

To do good thing in the world, first you must know who you are and what gives meaning to your life. —Robert Browning

· · · · ·

YOU JUST DON'T LUCK INTO THINGS AS MUCH AS YOU'D LIKE TO THINK YOU DO. YOU BUILD STEP BY STEP, WHETHER IT'S FRIENDSHIPS OR OPPORTUNITIES.

—Barbara Bush

· · · · ·

During my eighty-seven years I have witnessed a whole succession of technological revolutions. But none of them has done away with the need for character in the individual or the ability to think. —Bernard Mannes Baruch

· · · · ·

An inconvenience is only an adventure wrongly considered; an adventure is an inconvenience rightly considered.

—G. K. Chesterton

· · · · ·

It is the part of a wise man to keep himself to-day for to-morrow, and not to venture all his eggs in one basket.

—Miguel de Cervantes

· · · · ·

To please everybody is impossible; were I to undertake it, I should probably please nobody. —George Washington

· · · · ·

Being a hero is about the shortest-lived profession on earth. —Will Rogers

Spoon feeding in the long run teaches us nothing but the shape of the spoon.

—E. M. Forster

· · · · ·

When clouds form in the skies we know that rain will follow but we must not wait for it. Nothing will be achieved by attempting to interfere with the future before the time is ripe. Patience is needed. —I Ching

Keep away from people who try to belittle your ambitions. Small people always do that, but the really great make you feel that you too, can become great. —Mark Twain

· · · · ·

IF I HAVE EVER MADE ANY VALUABLE DISCOVERIES, IT HAS BEEN OWING MORE TO PATIENT ATTENTION, THAN TO ANY OTHER TALENT.

—Sir Isaac Newton

· · · · ·

A good solution applied with vigor now is better than a perfect solution applied ten minutes later. —George Smith Patton, Jr.

· · · · ·

One day Alice came to a fork in the road and saw a Cheshire cat in a tree. "Which road do I take?" she asked. "Where do you want to go?" was his response. "I don't know," Alice answered. "Then," said the cat, "it doesn't matter." —Lewis Carroll

· · · · ·

It is a paradoxical but profoundly true and important principle of life that the most likely way to reach a goal is to be aiming not at that goal itself but at some more ambitious goal beyond it. —Arnold Joseph Toynbee

· · · · ·

It takes as much energy to wish as it does to plan.

—Eleanor Roosevelt

* * * * *

I not only use all the brains that I have, but all that I can borrow. —Woodrow Wilson

* * * * *

If a man will begin with certainties, he shall end in doubts; but if he will be content to begin with doubts he shall end in certainties. —Sir Francis Bacon

* * * * *

THEY SAY THAT TIME CHANGES THINGS, BUT YOU ACTUALLY HAVE TO CHANGE THEM YOURSELF. —Andy Warhol

* * * * *

One of the annoying things about believing in free will and individual responsibility is the difficulty of finding somebody to blame your problems on. And when you do find somebody, it's remarkable how often his picture turns up on your driver's license. —P. J. O'Rourke

* * * * *

It does not matter how slowly you go so long as you do not stop.

—Confucius

I learned much from my teachers, more from my books, and most from my mistakes. —Anonymous

· · · · ·

LEAD, FOLLOW, OR GET OUT OF THE WAY.
—Thomas Paine

· · · · ·

A wise man will make more opportunities than he finds.

—Sir Francis Bacon

· · · · ·

If you wish in this world to advance,
Your merits you're bound to enhance;
You must stir it and stump it,
and blow your own trumpet.
Or trust me, you haven't a chance. —Sir William S. Gilbert

· · · · ·

Leadership is solving problems. The day soldiers stop bringing you their problems is the day you have stopped leading them. They have either lost confidence that you can help or concluded you do not care. Either case is a failure of leadership. —Colin Powell

· · · · ·

Success is dependent on effort. —Sophocles

· · · · ·

It doesn't matter if a cat is black or white, so long as it catches mice. —Deng Xiaoping

. . . . .

A good objective of leadership is to help those who are doing poorly to do well and to help those who are doing well to do even better. —Jim Rohn

. . . . .

Clear your mind of can't. —Solon

. . . . .

THERE IS NO SUCH THING AS A "SELF-MADE" PERSON. . . . EVERYONE WHO HAS EVER DONE A KIND DEED FOR US, OR SPOKEN ONE WORD OF ENCOURAGEMENT TO US, HAS ENTERED INTO THE MAKE-UP OF OUR CHARACTER AND OF OUR THOUGHTS, AS WELL AS OUR SUCCESS.

—George Matthew Adams

. . . . .

. . . Give every man thy ear, but few thy voice;
Take each man's censure, but reserve thy judgment.
Costly thy habit as thy purse can buy . . .
Neither a borrower nor a lender be;
For loan oft loses both itself and friend,
And borrowing dulls the edge of husbandry. —William Shakespeare

. . . . .

Giving your son a skill is better than giving him one thousand pieces of gold. —Chinese proverb

· · · · ·

Progress, far from consisting in change, depends on retentiveness. When change is absolute there remains no being to improve and no direction is set for possible improvement: and when experience is not retained, as among savages, infancy is perpetual. Those who cannot remember the past are condemned to repeat it. —George Santayana

· · · · ·

The man who has no imagination has no wings. —Muhammad Ali

If nothing ever changed, there'd be no butterflies.
—Anonymous

· · · · ·

I love the man that can smile in trouble, that can gather strength from distress, and grow brave by reflection. 'Tis the business of little minds to shrink, but he whose heart is firm, and whose conscience approves his conduct, will pursue his principles unto death. —Thomas Paine

· · · · ·

IF YOU DON'T LIKE SOMETHING, CHANGE IT. IF YOU CAN'T CHANGE IT, CHANGE YOUR ATTITUDE. DON'T COMPLAIN.

—Maya Angelou

· · · · ·

I TRY TO DO THE RIGHT THING AT THE RIGHT TIME. THEY MAY JUST BE LITTLE THINGS, BUT USUALLY THEY MAKE THE DIFFERENCE BETWEEN WINNING AND LOSING.

—Kareem Abdul-Jabbar

. . . . .

Great deeds are usually wrought at great risks. —Herodotus

. . . . .

Prosperity depends more on wanting what you have than having what you want. —Geoffrey F. Abert

. . . . .

If it sounds too good to be true, it is. —Anonymous

. . . . .

Never esteem anything as of advantage to you that will make you break your word or lose your self-respect.

—Henry Brooks Adams

. . . . .

All things are difficult before they are easy. —Thomas Fuller

. . . . .

A subtle thought that is in error may yet give rise to fruitful inquiry that can establish truths of great value. —Isaac Asimov

· · · · ·

If money be not thy servant, it will be thy master. The covetous man cannot so properly be said to possess wealth, as that may be said to possess him. —Sir Francis Bacon

· · · · ·

You can get a lot farther with a kind word and a gun than a kind word alone.

—Al Capone

One of the things I learned the hard way was that it doesn't pay to get discouraged. Keeping busy and making optimism a way of life can restore your faith in yourself. —Lucille Ball

· · · · ·

In a hierarchy every employee tends to rise to his level of incompetence. —Laurence J. Peter (expressing the so-called Peter Principle)

· · · · ·

Power is not revealed by striking hard or often, but by striking true. —Honoré de Balzac

· · · · ·

Millions saw the apple fall, but Newton was the one who asked why. —Bernard Baruch

· · · · ·

Riches do not consist in the possession of treasures, but in the use made of them. —Napoléon Bonaparte

· · · · ·

What makes a good follower? The single most important characteristic may well be a willingness to tell the truth. In a world of growing complexity leaders are increasingly dependent on their subordinates for good information, whether the leaders want to hear it or not. Followers who tell the truth and leaders who listen to it are an unbeatable combination. —Warren G. Bennis

· · · · ·

A hunch is creativity trying to tell you something. —Frank Capra

· · · · ·

Any fool can make things bigger, more complex, and more violent. It takes a touch of genius—and a lot of courage—to move in the opposite direction. —Albert Einstein

· · · · ·

The person interested in success has to learn to view failure as a healthy, inevitable part of the process of getting to the top.

—Dr. Joyce Brothers

· · · · ·

Good judgment comes from experience, and experience usually comes from bad judgment. —Anonymous

. . . . .

Ah, but a man's reach should exceed his grasp—or what's a heaven for? —Robert Browning

. . . . .

THE WAY TO DEVELOP SELF-CONFIDENCE IS TO DO THE THING YOU FEAR AND GET A RECORD OF SUCCESSFUL EXPERIENCES BEHIND YOU. DESTINY IS NOT A MATTER OF CHANCE, IT IS A MATTER OF CHOICE; IT IS NOT A THING TO BE WAITED FOR, IT IS A THING TO BE ACHIEVED.

—William Jennings Bryan

. . . . .

Believe nothing merely because you have been told it. Do not believe what your teacher tells you merely out of respect for the teacher. But whatsoever, after due examination and analysis, you find to be kind, conducive to the good, the benefit, the welfare of all beings—that doctrine believe and cling to, and take it as your guide. —Buddha

. . . . .

When you follow your bliss . . . doors will open where you would not have thought there would be doors; and where there wouldn't be a door for anyone else. —Joseph Campbell

The man without a purpose is like a ship without a rudder—a waif, a nothing, a no man. Have a purpose in life and having it, throw such strength of mind and muscle into your work as God has given you. —Thomas Carlyle

· · · · ·

Perseverance alone does not assure success. No amount of stalking will lead to game in a field that has none. —I Ching

· · · · ·

For myself I am an optimist—it does not seem to be much use being anything else. —Sir Winston Churchill

Don't accept your dog's admiration as conclusive evidence that you are wonderful.
—Ann Landers

· · · · ·

Nothing in the world can take the place of persistence. Talent will not; nothing is more common than unsuccessful men with talent. Genius will not; unrewarded genius is almost a proverb. Education will not; the world is full of educated derelicts. Persistence and determination are omnipotent. —Calvin Coolidge

· · · · ·

IRON RUSTS FROM DISUSE; STAGNANT WATER LOSES IT PURITY AND IN COLD WEATHER BECOMES FROZEN; EVEN SO DOES INACTION SAP THE VIGOR OF THE MIND.

—Leonardo da Vinci

· · · · ·

Graduation Guidance

Remember? Four years or more of endless reading, writing, and studying, culminating in your first degree. Now what? Here are eleven brilliant words to the (newly) wise.

Indulge your imagination in every possible flight.
—Jane Austen

Act the way you'd like to be and soon you'll be the way you act.
—George W. Crane

Never work just for money or for power. They won't save your soul or help you sleep at night. —Marian Wright Edelman

The only failure is not to try.
—George Clooney

A champion is someone who gets up when he can't.
—Jack Dempsey

Success is not the key to happiness. Happiness is the key to success. If you love what you are doing, you will be successful.
—Albert Schweitzer

Shoot for the moon. Even if you miss, you'll land among the stars.
—Les Brown

Be yourself. The world worships the original.
—Ingrid Bergman

If one advances confidently in the direction of one's dreams, and endeavours to live the life which one has imagined, one will meet with a success unexpected in common hours. —Henry David Thoreau

Often you just have to rely on your intuition.
—Bill Gates

A strong, positive self-image is the best possible preparation for success. —Joyce Brothers

The only safe thing is to take a chance. Play safe and you are dead. Taking risks is the essence of good work, and the difference between safe and bold can only be defined by yourself since no one else knows for what you are hoping when you embark on anything. —Mike Nichols

· · · · ·

It is a common experience that a problem difficult at night is resolved in the morning after a committee of sleep has worked on it. —John Steinbeck

· · · · ·

SMALL OPPORTUNITIES ARE OFTEN THE BEGINNING OF GREAT ENTERPRISES.
—Demosthenes

· · · · ·

Failure is instructive. The person who really thinks learns quite as much from his failures as from his successes. —John Dewey

· · · · ·

When you have eliminated the impossible, that which remains, however improbable, must be the truth.

—Sir Arthur Conan Doyle

· · · · ·

You can't build a reputation on what you're going to do.

—Henry Ford

The most pathetic person in the world is someone who has sight, but has no vision.
—Helen Keller

Annual income twenty pounds, annual expenditure nineteen pounds and six, result happiness. Annual income twenty pounds, annual expenditure twenty pounds ought and six, result misery.

—Charles Dickens

• • • • •

Happiness is as a butterfly which, when pursued, is always beyond our grasp, but which if you will sit down quietly, may alight upon you. —Nathaniel Hawthorne

Nothing great was ever achieved without enthusiasm.

—Ralph Waldo Emerson

• • • • •

The world is full of willing people; some willing to work, the rest willing to let them. —Robert Frost

• • • • •

I respect the man who knows distinctly what he wishes. The greater part of all mischief in the world arises from the fact that men do not sufficiently understand their own aims. They have undertaken to build a tower, and spend no more labor on the foundation than would be necessary to erect a hut.

—Johann Wolfgang von Goethe

• • • • •

I HAVE THE SIMPLEST TASTES. I AM ALWAYS SATISFIED WITH THE BEST.

—Oscar Wilde

· · · · ·

We are wiser than we know. —Ralph Waldo Emerson

· · · · ·

I find the great thing in this world is not so much where we stand, as in what direction we are moving—we must sail sometimes with the wind and sometimes against it—but we must sail, and not drift, nor lie at anchor. —Oliver Wendell Holmes, Jr.

· · · · ·

EXPERIENCE IS NOT WHAT HAPPENS TO YOU, IT IS WHAT YOU DO WITH WHAT HAPPENS TO YOU.

—Aldous Huxley

· · · · ·

A man must be big enough to admit his mistakes, smart enough to profit from them, and strong enough to correct them.

—John C. Maxwell

· · · · ·

Nothing will ever be attempted if all possible objections must first be overcome. —Samuel Johnson

· · · · ·

There is only one success—to be able to spend your life in your own way. —Christopher Darlington Morley

· · · · ·

If I were asked to give what I consider the single most useful bit of advice for all humanity, it would be this: Expect trouble as an inevitable part of life. . . . Look it squarely in the eye, and say, I will be bigger than you. You cannot defeat me.

—Ann Landers

· · · · ·

The highest reward for a man's toil is not what he gets for it but what he becomes by it. —John Ruskin

· · · · ·

It takes as much stress to be a success as it does to be a failure. —Emilio James Trujillo

· · · · ·

THE GREATEST GLORY IN LIVING LIES NOT IN NEVER FALLING, BUT IN RISING EVERY TIME WE FALL.

—Nelson Mandela

· · · · ·

Imagination will often carry us to worlds that never were. But without it we go nowhere. —Carl Sagan

• • • • •

There is always an easy solution to every human problem— neat, plausible, and wrong. —H. L. Mencken

• • • • •

A timid person is frightened before a danger, a coward during the time, and a courageous person afterward.

—Jean Paul Friedrich Richter

The two most powerful warriors are patience and time.

—Leo Tolstoy

• • • • •

A habit cannot be tossed out the window; it must be coaxed down the stairs a step at a time. —Mark Twain

• • • • •

Everybody knows if you are too careful you are so occupied in being careful that you are sure to stumble over something.

—Gertrude Stein

• • • • •

A PROFESSIONAL IS A MAN WHO CAN DO HIS BEST AT A TIME WHEN HE DOESN'T PARTICULARLY FEEL LIKE IT.

—Alistair Cooke

Doing the best at this moment puts you in the best place for the next moment. —Oprah Winfrey

• • • • •

There are no menial jobs, only menial attitudes.

—William John Bennett

• • • • •

MISTAKES ARE THE PORTALS FOR DISCOVERY.

—James Joyce

• • • • •

The pupil who is never required to do what he cannot do, never does what he can do. —John Stuart Mill

• • • • •

Kind words are short and easy to speak, but their echoes are truly endless.
—Mother Teresa

There are two kinds of failures: those who thought and never did, and those who did and never thought.

—Laurence J. Peter

• • • • •

Merely having an open mind is nothing; the object of opening the mind, as of opening the mouth, is to shut it again on something solid. —G. K. Chesterton

• • • • •

Obstacles are those frightful things you see when you take your eyes off your goal. —Henry Ford

· · · · ·

Never tell people how to do things. Tell them what you want them to achieve, and they will surprise you with their ingenuity. —George Smith Patton, Jr.

· · · · ·

I WOULD RATHER FAIL IN A CAUSE THAT WILL ULTIMATELY TRIUMPH THAN TO TRIUMPH IN A CAUSE THAT WILL ULTIMATELY FAIL.

—Woodrow Wilson

· · · · ·

One should not increase, beyond what is necessary, the number of entities required to explain anything. —William of Occam (this principle of parsimony is known as "Occam's razor")

· · · · ·

Success usually comes to those who are too busy to be looking for it. —Henry David Thoreau

· · · · ·

Blessed is the man who, having nothing to say, abstains from giving us wordy evidence of the fact. —George Eliot

· · · · ·

Curiosity . . . endows the people who have it with a generosity in argument and a serenity in cheerful willingness to let life take the form it will. —Alistair Cooke

· · · · ·

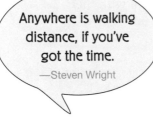

Anywhere is walking distance, if you've got the time.
—Steven Wright

When people keep telling you that you can't do a thing, you kind of like to try it.
—Margaret Chase Smith

· · · · ·

Never grow a wishbone where your backbone ought to be.
—Clementine Paddleford

Nobody can make you feel inferior without your consent.

—Eleanor Roosevelt

· · · · · ·

You can be discouraged by failure—or you can learn from it. So go ahead and make mistakes. Make all you can. Because, remember that's where you'll find success. On the far side.

—Thomas Watson, Sr.

· · · · · ·

Commit yourself to a dream. . . . Nobody who tries to do something great but fails is a total failure. Why? Because he can always rest assured that he succeeded in life's most important battle—he defeated the fear of trying.

—Robert H. Schuller

· · · · · ·

I AM ALWAYS DOING THAT WHICH I CAN NOT DO, IN ORDER THAT I MAY LEARN HOW TO DO IT.

—Pablo Picasso

· · · · · ·

There is nothing more difficult to take in hand, more perilous to conduct, or more uncertain in its success, than to take the lead in the introduction of a new order to things.

—Niccolò Machiavelli

· · · · · ·

Ambition can creep as well as soar. —Edmund Burke

· · · · ·

A JEST'S PROSPERITY LIES IN THE EAR OF HIM THAT HEARS IT, NEVER IN THE TONGUE OF HIM THAT MAKES IT.
—William Shakespeare

· · · · ·

If we work upon marble, it will perish; if we work upon brass, time will efface it; if we rear temples, they will crumble into dust; but if we work upon immortal minds and instill into them just principles, we are then engraving that upon tablets which no time will efface, but will brighten and brighten to all eternity. —Daniel Webster

· · · · ·

They can do all because they think they can. —Virgil

· · · · ·

White. A blank page or canvas. So many possibilities.
—Stephen Sondheim

· · · · ·

People have been known to achieve more as a result of working with others than against them. —Dr. Allan Fromme

· · · · ·

Trust yourself. You know more than you think you do.

—Benjamin Spock

. . . . .

For everything you have missed, you have gained something else. —Ralph Waldo Emerson

. . . . .

I WOULD SOONER FAIL THAN NOT BE AMONG THE GREATEST.

—John Keats

. . . . .

When the will defies fear, when the heart applauds the brain, when duty throws the gauntlet down to fate, when honor scorns to compromise with death—this is heroism.

—Robert Ingersoll

. . . . .

Let fear be a counselor and not a jailer. —Anthony Robbins

. . . . .

I am the wisest man alive, for I know one thing, and that is that I know nothing.

—Socrates

Chapter 4
A Learning Faculty

Utilize *your mind and allow it to grow. And for every grain of wisdom gained allow in a smidgen of fun. The selection of quotes contained in this chapter is sure to get your neurons firing.*

Cogito ergo sum. (I think, therefore I am.) —René Descartes

· · · · ·

Nothing else in the world . . . not all the armies . . . is so powerful as an idea whose time has come. —Victor Hugo

· · · · ·

We are shaped by our thoughts. We become what we think.

—Buddha

· · · · ·

I'D RATHER LEARN FROM ONE BIRD HOW TO SING THAN TO TEACH TEN THOUSAND STARS HOW NOT TO DANCE.

—e. e. cummings

If we value the pursuit of knowledge, we must be free to follow wherever that search may lead us. The free mind is no barking dog to be tethered on a one-foot chain. —Theodor Adorno

· · · · ·

Knowledge is power. —Sir Francis Bacon

· · · · ·

It is impossible to defeat an ignorant man in argument.
—William G. McAdoo

· · · · ·

KNOWLEDGE CAN BE CONVEYED, BUT NOT WISDOM. IT CAN BE FOUND, IT CAN BE LIVED, IT IS POSSIBLE TO BE CARRIED BY IT, MIRACLES CAN BE PERFORMED WITH IT, BUT IT CANNOT BE EXPRESSED IN WORDS AND TAUGHT.
—Herman Hesse

· · · · ·

Skepticism is the chastity of the intellect, and it is shameful to surrender it too soon or to the first comer: there is nobility in preserving it coolly and proudly through long youth, until at last, in the ripeness of instinct and discretion, it can be safely exchanged for fidelity and happiness. —George Santayana

· · · · ·

It is the mark of an educated mind to be able to entertain a thought without accepting it. —Aristotle

. . . . . .

Others have been here before me, and I walk in their footsteps. The books I have read were composed by generations of fathers and sons, mothers and daughters, teachers and disciples. I am the sum total of their experiences, their quests. And so are you. —Elie Wiesel

. . . . . .

The great instrument of moral good is the imagination.

—Percy Bysshe Shelley

. . . . . .

The test of a first-rate intelligence is the ability to hold two opposed ideas in the mind at the same time, and still retain the ability to function. One should, for example, be able to see that things are hopeless and yet be determined to make them otherwise. —F. Scott Fitzgerald

. . . . . .

HUMOR IS A SERIOUS THING. I LIKE TO THINK OF IT AS ONE OF OUR GREATEST EARLIEST NATURAL RESOURCES, WHICH MUST BE PRESERVED AT ALL COST.

—James Thurber

. . . . . .

When you read a classic you do not see in the book more than you did before. You see more in you than there was before.

—Clifton Fadiman

· · · · · ·

Mediocrity knows nothing higher than itself, but talent instantly recognizes genius. —Sir Arthur Conan Doyle

· · · · · ·

Life beats down and crushes the soul, but art reminds you that you have one. —Stella Adler

· · · · · ·

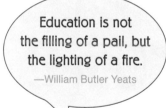

Education is not the filling of a pail, but the lighting of a fire.
—William Butler Yeats

I do not feel obliged to believe that that same God who has endowed us with sense, reason, and intellect has intended us to forgo their use. —Galileo Galilei

· · · · · ·

Exuberance is beauty. —William Blake

· · · · · ·

Writing is a struggle against silence. —Carlos Fuentes

· · · · · ·

Talk sense to a fool and he calls you foolish. —Euripides

YOU CANNOT TEACH A MAN ANYTHING; YOU CAN ONLY HELP HIM FIND IT WITHIN HIMSELF.

—Galileo Galilei

· · · · ·

I have always thought the actions of men the best interpreters of their thoughts. —John Locke

· · · · ·

People demand freedom of speech to make up for the freedom of thought which they avoid. —Søren Kierkegaard

· · · · ·

Anyone who conducts an argument by appealing to authority is not using his intelligence; he is just using his memory.

—Leonardo da Vinci

· · · · ·

Where so many hours have been spent in convincing myself that I am right, is there not some reason to fear I may be wrong? —Jane Austen

· · · · ·

Prejudices, it is well known, are most difficult to eradicate from the heart whose soil has never been loosened or fertilized by education; they grow there, firm as weeds among rocks. —Charlotte Brontë

The test and the use of man's education is that he finds pleasure in the exercise of his mind. —Jacques Martin Barzun

· · · · ·

I find that a great part of the information I have was acquired by looking up something and finding something else on the way. —Franklin P. Adams

· · · · ·

The writer wants to be understood much more than he wants to be respected or praised or even loved. And that perhaps, is what makes him different from others. —Leo C. Rosten

· · · · ·

Fantasy, abandoned by reason, produces impossible monsters; united with it, she is the mother of the arts and the origin of marvels. —Francisco de Goya

· · · · ·

PARADOXICALLY THOUGH IT MAY SEEM, IT IS NONE THE LESS TRUE THAT LIFE IMITATES ART FAR MORE THAN ART IMITATES LIFE.
—Oscar Wilde

· · · · ·

Genius is nothing but a great aptitude for patience.
—George-Louis de Buffon

Mindful Bites
The Top 10 Bits of Wisdom on the Art of Learning

If you have knowledge, let others light their candles in it.
—Margaret Fuller

The only real mistake is the one from which we learn nothing.
—John Powell

Try to learn something about everything and everything about something.
—Thomas Henry Huxley

The proof that you know something is that you are able to teach it.
—Aristotle

Learn as though you would never be able to master it; hold it as though you would be in fear of losing it —Confucius

You never know what is enough unless you know what is more than enough.
—William Blake

Never seem wiser, nor more learned, than the people you are with. Wear your learning, like your watch, in a private pocket, and do not merely pull it out and strike it merely to show that you have one. —Lord Chesterfield

Acquire new knowledge whilst thinking over the old, and you may become a teacher of others. —Confucius

Study as if you were going to live forever; live as if you were going to die tomorrow.
—Maria Mitchaell

The man who does not read good books has no advantage over the man who cannot read them.
—Mark Twain

People are always so boring when they band together. You have to be alone to develop all the idiosyncrasies that make a person interesting. —Andy Warhol

· · · · ·

Creative minds have been known to survive any sort of bad training. —Anna Freud

· · · · ·

AN INTELLECTUAL IS A MAN WHO SAYS A SIMPLE THING IN A DIFFICULT WAY; AN ARTIST IS A MAN WHO SAYS A DIFFICULT THING IN A SIMPLE WAY.
—Charles Bukowski

· · · · ·

Conception, my boy, fundamental brain work, is what makes all the difference in art. The job of the artist is always to deepen the mystery. —Francis Bacon

· · · · ·

Art is made to disturb. Science reassures. There is only one valuable thing in art: the thing you cannot explain.
—Georges Braque

· · · · ·

Precision is not reality. —Henri Matisse

· · · · ·

The purpose of art is to lay bare the questions which have been hidden by the answers. —James Baldwin

· · · · ·

The invariable mark of wisdom is to see the miraculous in the common. —Ralph Waldo Emerson

· · · · ·

Life is brief, art is long. —Hippocrates

· · · · ·

Poor is the pupil who does not surpass his master.

—Leonardo da Vinci

· · · · ·

Lord, grant that I may always desire more than I can accomplish. —Michelangelo

· · · · ·

Creativity is allowing yourself to make mistakes. Art is knowing which ones to keep. —Scott Adams

· · · · ·

In every man's heart there is a secret nerve that answers to the vibrations of beauty. —Christopher Darlington Morley

· · · · ·

BEAUTY IN THINGS LIES IN THE MIND
WHICH CONTEMPLATES THEM.

—David Hume

· · · · ·

The best and most beautiful things in life cannot be seen, nor touched, but are felt in the heart. —Helen Keller

· · · · ·

God, give us the grace to accept with serenity the things that cannot be changed, courage to change the things which should be changed, and the wisdom to distinguish the one from the other. —Reinhold Niebuhr

· · · · ·

There are flowers everywhere, for those who bother to look.
—Henri Matisse

Do not say a little in many words but a great deal in a few. —Pythagorus

· · · · ·

What sculpture is to a block of marble, education is to the soul.

—Joseph Addison

· · · · ·

Real education should educate us out of self into something far finer; into a selflessness which links us with all humanity.

—Lady Nancy Astor

· · · · ·

To educate a man is to unfit him to be a slave. —Frederick Douglass

· · · · ·

By words the mind is winged. —Aristophanes

· · · · ·

NO MAN CAN BE CALLED FRIENDLESS WHEN HE HAS GOD AND THE COMPANIONSHIP OF GOOD BOOKS.

—Elizabeth Barrett Browning

· · · · ·

Wise men talk because they have something to say; fools talk because they have to say something. —Saul Bellow

· · · · ·

A little learning is a dangerous thing / Drink deep, or taste not the Pierian spring. —Alexander Pope

· · · · ·

Be not a slave of words. —Thomas Carlyle

. . . . .

The confidence of ignorance will always overcome indecision of knowledge. —Anonymous

. . . . .

INTEGRITY WITHOUT KNOWLEDGE IS WEAK AND USELESS, AND KNOWLEDGE WITHOUT INTEGRITY IS DANGEROUS AND DREADFUL.
—Samuel Johnson

. . . . .

Beware the man of a single book. —Bertrand Russell

All wish to possess knowledge, but few, comparatively speaking, are willing to pay the price. —Juvenal

. . . . .

What really knocks me out is a book that, when you're all done reading it, you wish the author that wrote it was a terrific friend of yours and you could call him up on the phone whenever you felt like it. That doesn't happen much, though.
—J. D. Salinger

. . . . .

GENIUS MAY HAVE ITS LIMITATIONS, BUT STUPIDITY IS NOT THUS HANDICAPPED.

—L. Ron Hubbard

· · · · ·

He that studieth revenge keepeth his own wounds green, which otherwise would heal and do well. —John Milton

The first man to use abusive language instead of his fists was the founder of civilization. —Sigmund Freud

· · · · ·

It requires wisdom to understand wisdom; the music is nothing if the audience is deaf. —Walter Lippman

· · · · ·

Happy the man who has broken the chains which hurt the mind, and has given up worrying, once and for all. —Ovid

· · · · ·

If you make people think they're thinking, they'll love you; but if you really make them think, they'll hate you.

—Donald Robert Perry Marquis

· · · · ·

To act with common sense, according to the moment, is the best wisdom I know and the best philosophy is to do one's duties, take the world as it comes, submit respectfully to one's lot; bless the goodness that has given us so much happiness with it, whatever it is; and despise affectation. —Horace Walpole

· · · · ·

He who asks is a fool for five minutes, but he who does not ask remains a fool forever. —Chinese proverb

Human history becomes more and more a race between education and catastrophe.

—H. G. Wells

· · · · ·

A good listener is not only popular everywhere, but after a while he gets to know something. —Wilson Mizner

· · · · ·

Education makes a people easy to lead, but difficult to drive; easy to govern but impossible to enslave. —Lord Henry Brougham

· · · · ·

A correct answer is like an affectionate kiss.

—Johann Wolfgang von Goethe

· · · · ·

WISDOM IS NOT A PRODUCT OF SCHOOLING BUT OF THE LIFELONG ATTEMPT TO ACQUIRE IT.

—Albert Einstein

A teacher affects eternity; he can never tell, where his influence stops. —Henry Adams

· · · · ·

To teach is to learn twice. —Joseph Joubert

· · · · ·

DO NOT QUENCH YOUR INSPIRATION AND YOUR IMAGINATION; DO NOT BECOME THE SLAVE OF YOUR MODEL.
—Vincent van Gogh

· · · · ·

Style can make complicated things seem simple, or simple things complicated. —Jean Cocteau

· · · · ·

Fashions change, but style is forever. —Anonymous

· · · · ·

The conventional view serves to protect us from the painful job of thinking. —John Kenneth Galbraith

· · · · ·

The mind is its own place, and in itself, can make heaven of Hell, and a hell of Heaven. —John Milton

Youthful Teachings
10 Ways to Walk the Right Path

We parents can pass on far more than just eye color and curly hair; here are our favorite morsels for putting Junior on the right road.

Trust should be the basis for all our moral training. —Sir Robert Baden-Powell

Education is only the ladder with which to gather fruit from the tree of knowledge, not the fruit itself. —Anonymous

Correction does much, but encouragement does more. Encouragement after censure is as the sun after a shower.
—Johann Wolfgang Von Goethe

In youth we learn; in age we understand. —Marie von Ebner Eschenbach

A foolish consistency is the hobgoblin of little minds.
—Ralph Waldo Emerson

To bring up a child in the way he should go, travel that way yourself once in a while. —Josh Billings

Nothing is more important for the public welfare than to form and train our youth in wisdom and virtue. —Benjamin Franklin

Parents must get across the idea that "I love you always, but sometimes I do not love your behavior."
—Amy Vanderbilt

Teach thy tongue to say "I do not know," and thou shalt progress.
—Maimonides

Never help a child with a task at which he feels he can succeed.
—Maria Montessori

We should be careful to get out of an experience only the wisdom that is in it—and stop there; lest we be like the cat that sits down on a hot stove-lid. She will never sit down on a hot stove-lid again—and that is well; but also she will never sit down on a cold one anymore. —Mark Twain

· · · · ·

A MAN THINKS THAT BY MOUTHING HARD WORDS HE UNDERSTANDS HARD THINGS.
—Herman Melville

· · · · ·

Truth in science can be defined as the working hypothesis best suited to open the way to the next better one. —Konrad Lorenz

· · · · ·

I quote others only in order the better to express myself.
—Michel de Montaigne

· · · · ·

It is better to be high-spirited even though one makes more mistakes, than to be narrow-minded and too prudent.
—Vincent van Gogh

· · · · ·

Poetry begins in delight and ends in wisdom. —Robert Frost

· · · · ·

THERE IS NO SQUABBLING SO VIOLENT AS THAT BETWEEN PEOPLE WHO ACCEPTED AN IDEA YESTERDAY AND THOSE WHO WILL ACCEPT THE SAME IDEA TOMORROW.

—Christopher Darlington Morley

· · · · ·

A great memory is never made synonymous with wisdom, any more than a dictionary would be called a treatise.

—John Henry Newman

· · · · ·

Wisdom is ofttimes nearer when we stoop / Than when we soar. —William Wordsworth

· · · · ·

True wit is nature to advantage dressed, / What oft was thought, but ne'er so well expressed. —Alexander Pope

· · · · ·

It is a good thing for an uneducated man to read books of quotations. Bartlett's Familiar Quotations is an admirable work, and I studied it intently. The quotations when engraved upon the memory give you good thoughts. They also make you anxious to read the authors and look for more.

—Sir Winston Churchill

· · · · ·

To be positive:
To be mistaken at the
top of one's voice.

—Ambrose Bierce

Almost every wise saying has an opposite one, no less wise, to balance it.

—George Santayana

· · · · ·

Complaint always comes back in an echo from the ends of the world; but silence strengthens us. —G. K. Chesterton

There lives more faith in honest doubt, believe me, than in half the creeds. —Alfred, Lord Tennyson

· · · · ·

The ultimate result of shielding men from the effects of folly, is to fill the world with fools. —Herbert Spencer

· · · · ·

The liar's punishment is not in the least that he is not believed, but that he cannot believe anyone else.

—George Bernard Shaw

Contradiction is not a sign of falsity, nor the lack of contradiction a sign of truth. —Blaise Pascal

· · · · · ·

I do not agree with what you say, but I will defend to the death your right to say it. —Voltaire

· · · · · ·

I never know whether to pity or congratulate a man on coming to his senses. —William Makepeace Thackeray

· · · · · ·

Some books are undeservedly forgotten; none are undeservedly remembered. —W. H. Auden

· · · · · ·

True words are not always pretty; pretty words are not always true. —Anonymous

· · · · · ·

A man may learn wisdom even from a foe.
—Aristophanes

Truth lies within a little and certain compass, but error is immense.

—Henry St. John

· · · · · ·

A belief is not true because it is useful. —Henri Frédéric Amiel

Never chase a lie. Let it alone, and it will run itself to death.

—Lyman Beecher

· · · · ·

NOBODY CAN BE SO AMUSINGLY ARROGANT AS A YOUNG MAN WHO HAS JUST DISCOVERED AN OLD IDEA AND THINKS IT IS HIS OWN.

—Sydney Harris

· · · · ·

The opposite of a correct statement is a false statement. The opposite of a profound truth may well be another profound truth. —Niels Bohr

· · · · ·

As scarce as truth is, the supply has always been in excess of the demand. —Josh Billings

· · · · ·

I do not believe today everything I believed yesterday; I wonder will I believe tomorrow everything I believe today.

—Matthew Arnold

· · · · ·

A belief is not merely an idea the mind possesses; it is an idea that possesses the mind. —Robert Oxton Bolt

· · · · ·

When a man you like switches from what he said a year ago, or four years ago, he is a broad-minded person who has courage enough to change his mind with changing conditions. When a man you don't like does it, he is a liar who has broken his promises.

—Franklin P. Adams

· · · · ·

A lie gets halfway around the world before the truth has a chance to get its pants on. —Sir Winston Churchill

· · · · ·

Human reason is like a drunken man on horseback; set it up on one side and it tumbles over on the other. —Martin Luther

· · · · ·

I passionately hate the idea of being with it, I think an artist has always to be out of step with his time. —Orson Welles

· · · · ·

Any great work of art revives and readapts time and space, and the measure of its success is the extent to which it makes you an inhabitant of that world—the extent to which it invites you in and lets you breathe its strange, special air.

—Leonard Bernstein

· · · · ·

Truth that's told with bad intent / Beats all the Lies you can invent. —William Blake

· · · · ·

Man's mind, once stretched by a new idea, never regains its original dimensions. —Oliver Wendell Holmes, Jr.

Don't talk unless you can improve the silence. —Jorge Luis Borges

· · · · ·

The wastebasket is the writer's best friend. —Isaac Bashevis Singer

· · · · ·

Where is the wisdom we have lost in knowledge? Where is the knowledge we have lost in information? —T. S. Eliot

· · · · ·

THOSE WHO DREAM BY NIGHT IN THE DUSTY RECESSES OF THEIR MINDS WAKE IN THE DAY TO FIND THAT ALL WAS VANITY, BUT THE DREAMERS OF THE DAY ARE DANGEROUS MEN FOR THEY MAY ACT THEIR DREAM WITH OPEN EYES AND MAKE IT POSSIBLE.

—T. E. Lawrence

· · · · ·

Those who will not reason are bigots, those who cannot are fools, and those who dare not are slaves.

—George Gordon, Lord Byron

. . . . .

The power of accurate observation is commonly called cynicism by those who have not got it. —George Bernard Shaw

Heard melodies are sweet, but those unheard / Are sweeter . . .

—John Keats

. . . . .

DO NOT THE MOST MOVING MOMENTS OF OUR LIVES FIND US ALL WITHOUT WORDS?

—Marcel Marceau

. . . . .

It is only by introducing the young to great literature, drama and music, and to the excitement of great science that we open to them the possibilities that lie within the human spirit— enable them to see visions and dream dreams. —Eric Anderson

. . . . .

Only our individual faith
in freedom can keep us free.

—Dwight D. Eisenhower

Chapter 5

Politics and Politicians

Politicians are like parrots, they can be trained to say smart things, as evidenced by the quotes in this chapter.

We the People of the United States, in order to form a more perfect union, establish justice, insure domestic tranquility, provide for the common defense, promote the general welfare, and secure the blessings of liberty to ourselves and our posterity, do ordain and establish this Constitution for the United States of America.
—Preamble to the Constitution of the United States of America

· · · · · ·

We hold these Truths to be self-evident, that all Men are created equal, that they are endowed by their Creator with certain unalienable Rights, that among these are Life, Liberty and the Pursuit of Happiness . . . —Declaration of Independence

· · · · · ·

I have sworn upon the altar of God, eternal hostility against every form of tyranny over the mind of man. —Thomas Jefferson

All the great things are simple, and many can be expressed in a single word: freedom; justice; honor; duty; mercy; hope.

—Sir Winston Churchill

· · · · ·

Is life so dear, or peace so sweet, as to be purchased at the price of chains and slavery? Forbid it, Almighty God! I know not what course others may take; but as for me, give me liberty or give me death! —Patrick Henry

· · · · ·

Those who expect to reap the blessings of freedom must, like men, undergo the fatigue of supporting it. —Thomas Paine

· · · · ·

Power tends to corrupt, and absolute power corrupts absolutely.

—Lord Acton

· · · · ·

GOOD ORDER IS THE FOUNDATION OF ALL THINGS.

—EDMUND BURKE

· · · · ·

Give me the liberty to know, to utter, and to argue freely according to my conscience, above all liberties. —John Milton

· · · · ·

All politics is local. —Thomas P. "Tip" O'Neill

. . . . . .

They that can give up essential liberty to obtain a little temporary safety deserve neither liberty nor safety.

—Benjamin Franklin

. . . . . .

If you once forfeit the confidence of your fellow citizens, you can never regain their respect and esteem. You may fool all of the people some of the time; you can even fool some of the people all the time; but you can't fool all of the people all of the time. —Abraham Lincoln

. . . . . .

The language of the law must not be foreign to the ears of those who are to obey it. —Learned Hand

. . . . . .

The conquer'd, also, and enslaved by war, Shall, with their freedom lost, all virtue lose. —John Milton

. . . . . .

Politics is the art of looking for trouble, finding it whether it exists or not, diagnosing it incorrectly, and applying the wrong remedy. —Ernest Benn

. . . . . .

The hardest thing about any political campaign is how to win without proving that you are unworthy of winning.

—Theodor Adorno

· · · · ·

A society of sheep must in time beget a government of wolves.

—Bertrand de Jouvenel

· · · · ·

If we do not believe in freedom of speech for those we despise we do not believe in it at all. —Noam Chomsky

· · · · ·

Most people do not really want freedom, because freedom involves responsibility, and most people are frightened of responsibility. —Sigmund Freud

· · · · ·

You can only protect your liberties in this world by protecting the other man's freedom. You can only be free if I am free.

—Clarence Darrow

· · · · ·

All that is necessary for the triumph of evil is that good men do nothing.

—Edmund Burke

The buck stops here.

—Harry S Truman

· · · · ·

A leader or a man of action in a crisis almost always acts subconsciously and then thinks of the reasons for his action.

—Jawaharlal Nehru

· · · · ·

Mankind is at its best when it is most free. This will be clear if we grasp the principle of liberty. We must recall that the basic principle of liberty is freedom of choice, which saying many have on their lips but few in their minds. —Dante Alighieri

If liberty means anything at all, it means the right to tell people what they do not want to hear.

—George Orwell

· · · · ·

The first method for estimating the intelligence of a ruler is to look at the men he has around him. —Niccolò Machiavelli

· · · · ·

Being powerful is like being a lady. If you have to tell people you are—you aren't. —Margaret Thatcher

· · · · ·

WHO CONTROLS THE PAST CONTROLS THE FUTURE. WHO CONTROLS THE PRESENT CONTROLS THE PAST.

—George Orwell

· · · · ·

It is better to die on your feet than to live on your knees.

—Emiliano Zapata

. . . . .

YOU CAN DISCOVER WHAT YOUR ENEMY FEARS MOST BY OBSERVING THE MEANS HE USES TO FRIGHTEN YOU.

—Eric Hoffer

. . . . .

The very essence of a free government consists in considering offices as public trusts, bestowed for the good of the country, and not for the benefit of an individual or a party.

—John C. Calhoun

. . . . .

The free, exploring mind of the individual human is the most valuable thing in the world. And this I would fight for: the freedom of the mind to take any direction it wishes, undirected. And this I must fight against: any idea, religion, or government which limits or destroys the individual.

—John Steinbeck

. . . . .

Justice delayed is justice denied. —Legal maxim

. . . . .

I only ask to be free. The butterflies are free. —Charles Dickens

The Art of Presidential Sparring
The Best of Debating Through History

He has no more backbone than a chocolate éclair.

—Theodore Roosevelt on William McKinley

A rigid, fanatic, ambitious, selfishly partisan and sectional turncoat with too much genius and too little common sense, who will either die a traitor or a madman.

—Henry Clay on John C. Calhoun

He is vain, irritable, and a bad calculator of the force and probable effect of the motives which govern men.

—Thomas Jefferson on John Adams

He is the most dangerous man of the age.

—Woodrow Wilson on Theodore Roosevelt

A barbarian who cannot write a sentence of grammar and can hardly spell his name.

—John Quincy Adams on Andrew Jackson

His disposition is as perverse and mulish as that of his father.

—James Buchanan on John Quincy Adams

He is a bewildered, confounded, and miserably perplexed man.

—Abraham Lincoln on James Polk

He's a nice guy, but he played too much football with his helmet off.

—Lyndon B. Johnson on Gerald Ford

When I was president, I said I was a Ford, not a Lincoln. Well, what we have now is a convertible Dodge.

—Gerald Ford on Bill Clinton

Ike didn't know anything, and all the time he was in office, he didn't learn a thing . . . The general doesn't know any more about politics than a pig knows about Sunday.

—Harry S Truman on Dwight D. Eisenhower

The true greatness of nations is in those qualities which constitute the greatness of the individual. —Charles Sumner

· · · · ·

The best use of laws is to teach men to trample bad laws under their feet. —Wendell Phillips

· · · · ·

NO MAN IS ABOVE THE LAW AND NO MAN IS BELOW IT; NOR DO WE ASK ANY MAN'S PERMISSION WHEN WE REQUIRE HIM TO OBEY IT. OBEDIENCE OF THE LAW IS DEMANDED; NOT ASKED AS A FAVOR.

—Theodore Roosevelt

· · · · ·

We hold these truths to be self-evident, that all men and women are created equal. —Elizabeth Cady Stanton

· · · · ·

No taxation without representation.

—Rallying cry of the American Revolution

· · · · ·

I must study politics and war that my sons may have liberty to study mathematics and philosophy. —John Adams

A people that values its privileges above its principles soon loses both. —Dwight D. Eisenhower

. . . . .

The death of democracy is not likely to be an assassination from ambush. It will be a slow extinction from apathy, indifference, and undernourishment. —Robert Hutchins

. . . . .

The right to be heard does not automatically include the right to be taken seriously. —Hubert H. Humphrey

. . . . .

It is inaccurate to say I hate everything. I am strongly in favor of common sense, common honesty, and common decency. This makes me forever ineligible for any public office.

—H. L. Mencken

. . . . .

Freedom of thought and the right to private judgment, in matters of conscience, driven from every corner of the earth, direct their course to this happy country as their last asylum. Let us cherish the noble guests, and shelter them under the wings of universal toleration. —Samuel Adams

. . . . .

Those who corrupt the public mind are just as evil as those who steal from the public purse. —Adlai E. Stevenson

· · · · ·

There are few things wholly evil or wholly good. Almost everything, especially of government policy, is an inseparable compound of the two, so that our best judgment of the preponderance between them is continually demanded.

—Abraham Lincoln

· · · · ·

A man's feet should be planted in his country, but his eyes should survey the world. —George Santayana

· · · · ·

I expose slavery in this country, because to expose it is to kill it. Slavery is one of those monsters of darkness to whom the light of truth is death. —Frederick Douglass

· · · · ·

Nothing in life is certain except death and taxes.
—Benjamin Franklin

The true republic: men, their rights and nothing more; women, their rights and nothing less. —Franklin P. Adams

· · · · ·

I know not with what weapons World War III will be fought, but World War IV will be fought with sticks and stones.

—Albert Einstein

Practical politics consists in ignoring facts. —Henry Brooks Adams

· · · · ·

IN POLITICS STUPIDITY IS NOT A HANDICAP.

—Napoléon Bonaparte

· · · · ·

Even when laws have been written down, they ought not always to remain unaltered. —Aristotle

If mankind minus one were of one opinion, then mankind is no more justified in silencing the one than the one—if he had the power—would be justified in silencing mankind.

—John Stuart Mill

· · · · ·

ONE MAN WITH COURAGE IS A MAJORITY.

—Thomas Jefferson

· · · · ·

Toleration is good for all, or it is good for none. —Edmund Burke

· · · · ·

The Law, in its majestic equality, forbids the rich, as well as the poor, to sleep under the bridges, to beg in the streets, and to steal bread. —Anatole France

Presidential Advice
Lessons of Wisdom from the Commander in Chief

Forgive your enemies, but never forget their names.
—John F. Kennedy

Don't get mad. Don't get even. Just get elected, then get even.
—James Carville

Get action. Do things; be sane, don't fritter away your time; create, act, take a place wherever you are and be somebody; Get action. Seize the moment. Man was never intended to become an oyster.
—Theodore Roosevelt

To err is Truman.
—A popular joke in 1948

If you can't convince them, confuse them.
—Harry S Truman

You don't lead by hitting people over the head—that's assault, not leadership.
—Dwight D. Eisenhower

Never say no when a client asks for something, even if it is the moon. You can always try, and anyhow there is plenty of time afterwards to explain that it was not possible.
—Richard M. Nixon

If a dog will not come to you after having looked you in the face, you should go home and examine your conscience. —Woodrow Wilson

Cautious, careful people always casting about to preserve their reputation or social standards never can bring about reform. Those who are really in earnest are willing to be anything or nothing in the world's estimation, and publicly and privately, in season and out, avow their sympathies with despised ideas and their advocates, and bear the consequences. —Susan B. Anthony

・ ・ ・ ・ ・

Injustice anywhere is a threat to justice everywhere.

—Martin Luther King, Jr.

・ ・ ・ ・ ・

Let every nation know, whether it wishes us well or ill, that we shall pay any price, bear any burden, meet any hardship, support any friend, oppose any foe, in order to assure the survival and the success of liberty.

So let us begin anew—remembering on both sides that civility is not a sign of weakness, and sincerity is always subject to proof. Let us never negotiate out of fear. But let us never fear to negotiate. . . . And so, my fellow Americans: ask not what your country can do for you—ask what you can do for your country. —John F. Kennedy

・ ・ ・ ・ ・

The politician is . . . trained in the art of inexactitude. His words tend to be blunt or rounded, because if they have a cutting edge they may later return to wound him.

—Edward R. Murrow

・ ・ ・ ・ ・

Bad officials are elected by good citizens who do not vote.

—George Jean Nathan

· · · · ·

War is delightful to those who have had no experience of it.

—Desiderius Erasmus

· · · · ·

YOU CANNOT SIMULTANEOUSLY PREVENT AND PREPARE FOR WAR.

—Albert Einstein

· · · · ·

The nine most terrifying words in the English language are, "I'm from the government and I'm here to help." —Ronald Reagan

· · · · ·

If you can't stand the heat, get out of the kitchen. —Harry S Truman

· · · · ·

We learn from history that we do not learn from history.

—Georg Wilhelm Friedrich Hegel

Politicians are the same all over. They promise to build bridges even when there are no rivers. —Nikita Khrushchev

· · · · ·

One cool judgment is worth a dozen hasty councils. The thing to do is to supply light and not heat. —Woodrow Wilson

Rebellion to tyrants is obedience to God. —Thomas Jefferson

· · · · ·

If the misery of the poor be caused not by the laws of nature, but by our institutions, great is our sin.

—Charles Darwin

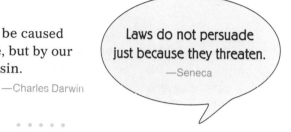

Laws do not persuade just because they threaten.
—Seneca

· · · · ·

The greatest dangers to liberty lurk in insidious encroachment by men of zeal, well-meaning, but without understanding.

—Louis D. Brandeis

· · · · ·

Freedom . . . is not ours by inheritance; it must be fought for and defended constantly by each generation, for it comes only once to a people. Those who have known freedom, and then lost it, have never known it again. —Ronald Reagan

· · · · ·

You have not converted a man because you have silenced him.

—Viscount John Morley

· · · · ·

I know war as few men now living know it, and nothing to me is more revolting. I have long advocated its complete abolition, as its very destructiveness on both friend and foe has rendered it useless as a means of settling international disputes. —General Douglas MacArthur

· · · · ·

The most effective way of attacking vice is to expose it to public ridicule. People can put up with rebukes, but they cannot bear being laughed at: they are prepared to be wicked but they dislike appearing ridiculous. —Molière

· · · · ·

If a nation values anything more than freedom, it will lose its freedom; and the irony of it is that if it is comfort or money that it values more, it will lose that too. —W. Somerset Maugham

· · · · ·

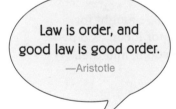

Law is order, and good law is good order. —Aristotle

Man does not live by words alone, despite the fact that sometimes he has to eat them. —Adlai E. Stevenson

· · · · ·

Freedom is not worth having if it does not connote freedom to err. It passes my comprehension how human beings, be they ever so experienced and able, can delight in depriving other human beings of that precious right. —Mohandas Gandhi

· · · · ·

The united voice of millions cannot lend the smallest foundation to falsehood. —Oliver Goldsmith

The punishment which the wise suffer who refuse to take part in the government, is to live under the government of worse men. —Plato

· · · · ·

When you are right, you cannot be too radical; When you are wrong, you cannot be too conservative. —Martin Luther King, Jr.

· · · · ·

A government that is big enough to give you all you want is big enough to take it all away. —Barry Goldwater

· · · · ·

The hottest places in hell are reserved for those who in times of great moral crises maintain their neutrality. —Dante Alighieri

· · · · ·

America will never be destroyed from the outside. If we falter and lose our freedoms, it will be because we destroyed ourselves. —Abraham Lincoln

· · · · ·

THE BASIS OF OUR POLITICAL SYSTEM IS THE RIGHT OF THE PEOPLE TO MAKE AND TO ALTER THEIR CONSTITUTIONS OF GOVERNMENT.

—George Washington

· · · · ·

At the end of the game,
the king and the pawn go
back in the same box.

—Italian proverb

Chapter 6

Proverbial Wisdom

You can't judge a book by its cover, or a man by the contents of his character. Who said that? Proverbs!

A country can be judged by the quality of its proverbs.

—German proverb

· · · · · ·

A handful of patience is worth more than a bushel of brains.

—Dutch proverb

· · · · · ·

It is easy to despise what you cannot get. —Aesop,"The Fox and the Grapes" (the origin of the phrase "sour grapes")

· · · · · ·

A bird in the hand is worth two in the bush. —English proverb

A quiet fool is half a sage.
—Yiddish proverb

· · · · ·

It is thrifty to prepare today for the wants of tomorrow.
—Aesop, "The Ant and the Grasshopper"

· · · · · ·

Union gives strength. —Aesop, "The Bundle of Sticks"

· · · · · ·

If you want to give God a good laugh, tell Him your plans.
—Yiddish proverb

· · · · · ·

PLEASE ALL, AND YOU WILL PLEASE NONE.
—Aesop, "The Man, the Boy, and the Donkey"

· · · · · ·

People often grudge others what they cannot enjoy themselves.
—Aesop, "The Dog in the Manger"

· · · · · ·

We often give our enemies the means of our own destruction.
—Aesop, "The Eagle and the Arrow"

· · · · · ·

It is easy to be brave from a safe distance. —Aesop, "The Wolf and the Kid"

· · · · · ·

Do not count your chickens before they are hatched.

—Aesop, "The Milk Woman and Her Pail"

- - - - - -

A JOURNEY OF A THOUSAND MILES BEGINS WITH A SINGLE STEP.

—Chinese proverb

- - - - -

Procrastination is the thief of time. —Proverb found in many cultures

- - - - -

Beware lest you lose the substance by grasping at the shadow.

—Aesop, "The Dog and the Shadow"

- - - - -

Luck is like having a rice dumpling fly into your mouth.

—Japanese proverb

- - - - -

THE BEST ARMOR IS TO KEEP OUT OF RANGE.

—Italian proverb

- - - - -

Men often applaud an imitation, and hiss the real thing.

—Aesop, "The Buffoon and the Countryman"

Profound Proverbs
15 Ancient Proverbs on the Way to a Good Life

A candle loses nothing by lighting another candle. —Italian

Good habits result from resisting temptation.

—Ancient

An ounce of patience is worth a pound of brains. —Dutch

No matter how far you have gone on the wrong road, turn back.

—Turkish

Even nectar is poison if taken in excess. —Hindu

Only your real friends will tell you when your face is dirty. —Sicilian

He who wants a rose must respect the thorn.

—Persian

How beautiful it is to do nothing, and then rest afterward.

—Spanish

With lies you may go ahead in the world, but you can never go back. —Russian

When you shoot an arrow of truth, dip its point in honey.

—Arabian

Life is an echo; what you send out comes back. —Chinese

If a man is as wise as a serpent, he can afford to be as harmless as a dove. —Cheyenne

Who goes a–borrowing, goes a–sorrowing.

—English

Never rely on the glory of the morning nor the smiles of your mother-in-law.

—Japanese

Don't be afraid to cry. It will free your mind of sorrowful thoughts. —Hopi

Better to light a candle than to curse the darkness.

—Chinese proverb

• • • • •

WHEN SPIDERS UNITE, THEY
CAN TIE DOWN A LION.

—Ethiopian proverb

• • • • •

Love is friendship set on fire. —French proverb

• • • • •

The death of a friend is equivalent to the loss of a limb.

—German proverb

• • • • •

Dance as if no one's watching, sing as if no one's listening, and live everyday as if it were your last. —Irish proverb

• • • • •

The reverse side also has a reverse side. —Japanese proverb

• • • • •

The older the fiddle, the sweeter the tune. —Irish proverb

• • • • •

VISION WITHOUT ACTION IS DAYDREAM.
ACTION WITHOUT VISION IS NIGHTMARE.

—Japanese proverb

· · · · ·

The generous and bold have the best lives. —Norwegian proverb

· · · · ·

Fear is only as deep as the mind allows. —Japanese proverb

· · · · ·

To be damned by the devil is to be truly blessed.

—Chinese proverb

· · · · ·

It is better to live one day as a lion,
than a thousand days as a lamb.

—Roman proverb

· · · · ·

He who allows his day to pass by
without practicing generosity and
enjoying life's pleasures is like a
blacksmith's bellows—he breathes
but does not live. —Sanskrit proverb

· · · · ·

Be humble for you are made of earth. Be noble for you are made of stars. —Serbian proverb

· · · · ·

It takes an entire village to raise a child —African proverb

Even a clock that does not work is right twice a day.
—Polish proverb

· · · · ·

Fear less, hope more; eat less, chew more; whine less, breathe more; talk less, say more; hate less, love more; and all good things are yours. —Swedish proverb

· · · · ·

Slow and steady wins the race. —Aesop, "The Tortoise and the Hare"

· · · · ·

By asking for the impossible, obtain the best possible.
—Italian proverb

· · · · ·

If you must play, decide on three things at the start: the rules of the game, the stakes, and the quitting time. —Chinese proverb

· · · · ·

He who hurries can not walk with dignity. —Chinese proverb

· · · · ·

Don't throw away the old bucket until you know whether the new one holds water. —Swedish proverb

. . . . .

It's the final straw that broke the camel's back. —English proverb

. . . . .

Tell me and I'll forget. Show me, and I may not remember. Involve me, and I'll understand. —Native American proverb

. . . . .

What's good for the goose is good for the gander.
—English proverb

. . . . .

HE WHO LIES DOWN WITH DOGS, RISES WITH FLEAS.
—English proverb

. . . . .

Time and words can't be recalled, even if it was only yesterday. —Estonian proverb

. . . . .

Too many cooks spoil the broth. —English proverb

. . . . .

You won't help shoots grow by pulling them up higher.

—Chinese proverb

. . . . .

Ask the experienced rather than the learned. —Arabic proverb

. . . . .

Tomorrow is often the busiest time of the year. —Spanish proverb

. . . . .

When I rest, I rust. —German proverb

Nobody's sweetheart is ugly.
—Dutch proverb

. . . . .

Revenge is a dish best served cold. —Italian proverb

. . . . .

He who is outside his door has the hardest part of his journey behind him. —Flemish proverb

. . . . .

Birds of a feather flock together. —English proverb

. . . . .

You can't hatch chickens from fried eggs. —German proverb

Trees often transplanted seldom prosper. —Flemish proverb

· · · · ·

Roasted pigeons will not fly into one's mouth. —Dutch proverb

· · · · ·

The early bird catches the worm. —English proverb

· · · · ·

ONE MEETS HIS DESTINY OFTEN IN THE ROAD HE TAKES TO AVOID IT.
—French proverb

· · · · ·

When the cat's away, the mice will play. —French proverb

· · · · ·

Curiosity killed the cat. —English proverb

· · · · ·

You can't dance at two weddings at the same time; nor can you sit on two horses with one behind. —Yiddish proverb

· · · · ·

Let sleeping dogs lie. —French proverb

Seasoned Sayings
The Clash of Nations

Sometimes, neighbors just can't get along, as these less-than-kind proverbs reveal.

A fighting Frenchman runs away from even a she-goat. —Russian

Spaniards are like lice: once they are there, it is difficult to get rid of them. —German

Marry a German and you'll see that the women have hairy tongues. —Romanian

If there is a Hell, Rome is built on top of it. —German

Cross yourself once before an Andalusian and thrice on spotting an Italian. —Spanish

The German may be a good fellow, but it is best to hang him just the same. —Russian

He who would eat in Spain must bring his kitchen along. —German

A Spaniard may be trusted, but no further than your nose. —German

There are only two kinds of Chinese—those who give bribes, and those who take them. —Russian

How can you tell a Russian? Go to sleep and he will rob you. —Ukrainian

The friendship of the French is like their wine, exquisite, but of short duration. —German

A demon took a monkey to wife—the results, by the grace of God, was the English. —Indian

If a Russian is in the hills, count your olives. —Greek

Better the devil in your house than a Russian. —Ukrainian

Half an Italian in a house is one too many. —German

When rats infest the palace, a lame cat is better than the swiftest horse. —Chinese proverb

· · · · ·

There are plenty more fish in the sea. —English proverb

· · · · ·

Whoever gossips to you will gossip about you.
—Spanish proverb

You can lead a horse to water, but you can't make him drink. —English proverb

· · · · ·

It's too late to close the stable door after the horse has bolted.
—French proverb

· · · · ·

Even the candle seller dies in the dark. —Colombian proverb

· · · · ·

A road to a friend's house is never long. —Danish proverb

· · · · ·

HE WHO DOES NOTHING MAKES NO MISTAKES.
—Italian proverb

· · · · ·

SPEAK SILVER, REPLY GOLD.

—Swahili proverb

· · · · ·

When one door shuts, a hundred open. —Spanish proverb

· · · · ·

The greedy man stores all but friendship. —Irish proverb

· · · · ·

If a little money does not go out, great money will not come in.

—Chinese proverb

· · · · ·

A people without history is like the wind on the buffalo grass.

—Lakota Sioux proverb

· · · · ·

Joy shared is twice the joy. Sorrow shared is half the sorrow.

—Swedish proverb

· · · · ·

A rich child often sits in a poor mother's lap. —Danish proverb

· · · · ·

A fool and his money are soon parted. —English proverb

· · · · ·

Worry gives a small thing a big shadow. —Swedish proverb

· · · · ·

Least said, soonest mended.

—Irish proverb

The gods help them that help themselves.

—Aesop, "Hercules and the Waggoner"

· · · · ·

Do not judge a man until you have walked two moons in his moccasins. —Native American proverb

· · · · ·

HOWEVER LONG THE NIGHT, THE DAWN WILL BREAK.

—African proverb

· · · · ·

PRIDE GOETH BEFORE DESTRUCTION, AND HAUGHTY SPIRIT BEFORE A FALL.

—The Bible, Proverbs 16:18

* * * * *

Appearances often are deceiving. —Aesop, "The Wolf and the Lamb"

* * * * *

Big mouthfuls often choke. —Italian proverb

* * * * *

Familiarity breeds contempt. —Aesop, "The Fox and the Lion"

* * * * *

If you want people to think you are wise, agree with them.

—Yiddish proverb

* * * * *

BLESSED IS THE MAN WHO CAN LAUGH AT HIMSELF, FOR HE WILL NEVER CEASE TO BE AMUSED.

—Proverb found in many cultures

* * * * *

Part II
Funniest

Things
Ever Said

· ·

Love, wisdom and success are wondrous things to have, but it also takes laughter to make life complete. No worries: On the pages ahead are best lines from some of the funniest people, guaranteed to make you smile, giggle, guffaw and just feel good.

I take my wife everywhere,
but she keeps finding
her way back.

—Henny Youngman

Chapter 7
The Practical Jokers

*G*iggles, guffaws, and knee-slappers make life wonderful. Here are dozens of hilarious moments from our funniest, favorite funny people.

Bob Hope

Bob Hope was the reigning stand-up comedian for much of the twentieth century, whether in movies, on radio and TV or entertaining the troops during wartime. His fixation with golf was an integral part of his life . . . and art.

· · · · ·

"Players occasionally have to contend with these gusty desert winds. I hit a ball into the wind one day . . . but I shouldn't have watched it with my mouth open. I'm the only guy around here with an Adam's Apple marked Spalding Kro-Flite.**"**

—on an incident that occurred to him one year at La Quinta
and left him speechless—if you can believe it

· · · · ·

"I set out to play golf with the intention of shooting my age, but I shot my weight instead.**"**

· · · · ·

"Incidentally, the toughest parts of the course for me nowadays are the sand traps. It's not hard to get the ball out . . . the problem is to get me out, at my age."

· · · · ·

I asked my good friend, Arnold Palmer, how I could improve my game, he advised me to cheat.
—Bob Hope

"I've played some strange rounds of golf in my travels. One course in Alaska was hacked out of the wilderness. My caddy was a moose. Every time I reached for a club he thought I was trying to steal his antlers."

· · · · ·

"The Scottish caddies are great. One old fellow at St. Andrews told me, "I had a golfer who was so lousy he threw his clubs into the water. Then he dived in himself. I thought he was going to drown, but I remembered he couldn't keep his head down long enough.""

· · · · ·

"You should have seen the Christmas cards I got this year. I got one card from Marilyn Monroe with a picture of her in a bathing suit. What a picture. You know how George Washington looks straight ahead on a two-cent stamp. Well, on this envelope, he kept peeking over his shoulder."

· · · · ·

"Oscar night at my house is called Passover."
—joking about the fact that he has never won an Oscar for his acting abilities

❝A James Cagney love scene is one where he lets the other guy live. ❞

· · · · ·

❝Jimmy Stewart could have been a good golfer, but he speaks so slowly that by the time he yells "Fore!" the guy he's hit is already in an ambulance on the way to the hospital. ❞

W. C. Fields

The legendary film, vaudeville, and radio curmudgeon and tippler with the bulbous nose and rotund body who said that "anyone who hates children and animals can't be all bad."

· · · · ·

❝W. C. Fields appeared on the program with ventriloquist Edgar Bergen with whose dummy, Charlie McCarthy, Fields had a running feud. Fields smuggled a saw on stage and, as a stunned Bergen looked on, finally cut his adversary down to size. "I'll always have a warm place for you, Charlie," Fields said.

"Where?" Charlie asked. "In your heart?"

"No, in my fireplace." ❞

· · · · ·

❝I was married once—in San Francisco. I haven't seen her for many years. The great earthquake and fire in 1906 destroyed the marriage certificate. There's no legal proof. Which proves that earthquakes aren't all bad. ❞

· · · · ·

"If at first you don't succeed, try, try, and try again. Then give up. There's no use being a damned fool about it."

A woman drove me to drink—and I hadn't even the courtesy to thank her.
—W. C. Fields

"Madam, there's no such thing as a tough child—if you parboil them first for seven hours, they always come out tender."

George Burns

With his wife Gracie Allen and his ever-present cigar, Burns was a popular figure on radio and TV, living to age 100 and working almost until his death.

I was married by a judge. I should have asked for a jury.
—George Burns

"First you forget names, then you forget faces. Next you forget to pull your zipper up and finally, you forget to pull it down."

"A good sermon should have a good beginning and a good ending, and they should be as close together as possible."

"Actually, it only takes one drink to get me loaded. Trouble is, I can't remember if it's the thirteenth or fourteenth."

❝Happiness? A good cigar, a good meal, a good cigar and a good woman—or a bad woman; it depends on how much happiness you can handle.❞

• • • • •

❝Jack [Benny] was tremendously talented, and I can honestly say I've never heard anyone play the violin the way he did. And I'll always be grateful for that, too.❞

Jack Benny

A star of radio and TV, Benny was well known for his supposed stinginess and less-than-virtuoso violin playing.

• • • • •

❝Jack Benny is walking down the street, when a stick-up man pulls out a gun and says, "Your money or your life!" An extremely long silence follows. "Your money or your life!" the thug repeats.

Finally, Benny says, "I'm thinking!"❞

• • • • •

❝I don't want to tell you how much insurance I carry with the Prudential, but all I can say is: when I go, they go too.❞

> I don't deserve this award, but I have arthritis and I don't deserve that either.
>
> —Jack Benny

• • • • •

❝Give me golf clubs, fresh air and a beautiful partner, and you can keep the clubs and the fresh air.❞

· · · · ·

❝It's a real Strad, you know. If it isn't I'm out one hundred and ten dollars. The reason I got it so cheap is that it's one of the few Strads made in Japan.❞ —about his fiddle

· · · · ·

❝Any man who would walk five miles through the snow, barefoot, just to return a library book so he could save three cents—that's my kind of guy.❞ —about Abraham Lincoln

Henny Youngman

The king of the one-liners, Youngman is best known for his "Take my wife . . . please!" signature joke.

· · · · ·

❝The patient says, "Doctor, it hurts when I do this."

The doctor replies, "Then don't do that!"❞

· · · · ·

"The doctor says to the patient, "Take your clothes off and stick your tongue out the window."

"What will that do?" asks the patient.

The doctor says, "I'm mad at my neighbor!""

. . . . .

"Getting on a plane, I told the ticket lady, "Send one of my bags to New York, send one to Los Angeles, and send one to Miami."

She said, "We can't do that!"

I told her, "You did it last week!""

. . . . .

"A father is explaining ethics to his son, who is about to go into business: "Suppose a woman comes in and orders a hundred dollars' worth of material. You wrap it up, and you give it to her. She pays you with a $100 bill. But as she goes out the door, you realize she's given you two $100 bills. Now, here's where the ethics come in: Should you or should you not tell your partner?""

Someone stole all my credit cards, but I won't be reporting it. The thief spends less than my wife did.

—Henny Youngman

. . . . .

"I asked my wife, "Where do you want to go for our anniversary?"

She said, "Somewhere I have never been!"

I told her, "How about the kitchen?""

. . . . .

Rodney Dangerfield

Dangerfield's nightclub routine was based on his "I don't get no respect" inferiority complex.

· · · · ·

"I went to the psychiatrist, and he says, "You're crazy."
I tell him I want a second opinion.
He says, "Okay, you're ugly too!""

· · · · ·

"I told my psychiatrist that everyone hates me. He said I was being ridiculous—everyone hasn't met me yet."

· · · · ·

> I tell ya when I was a kid, all I knew was rejection. My yo-yo, it never came back!
> —Rodney Dangerfield

"With my wife I don't get no respect. I made a toast on her birthday to "the best woman a man ever had." The waiter joined me."

· · · · ·

"What a childhood I had. Why, when I took my first step, my old man tripped me!"

· · · · ·

"With my dog I don't get no respect. He keeps barking at the front door. He don't want to go out. He wants me to leave."

· · · · ·

Zingers and Zowees!
Our Top Ten Favorite Comedic Insults

I'd call him a sadistic, hippophilic necrophile, but that would be beating a dead horse. —Woody Allen

He's so fat, he can be his own running mate. —Johnny Carson

She's got such a narrow mind, when she walks fast her earrings bang together. —John Cantu

It's like cuddling with a Butterball turkey. —Jeff Foxworthy

He has the mathematical abilities of a Clydesdale. —David Letterman

She got her good looks from her father. He's a plastic surgeon. —Groucho Marx

She's the kind of woman who climbed the ladder of success—wrong by wrong. —Mae West

Her hat is a creation that will never go out of style. It will look ridiculous year after year. —Fred Allen

Why are we honoring this man? Have we run out of human beings? —Milton Berle

His golf bag does not contain a full set of irons. —Robin Williams

"Last week I saw my psychiatrist. I told him, "Doc, I keep thinking I'm a dog." He told me to get off his couch."

· · · · ·

"I worked in a pet store and people kept asking how big I'd get."

Joan Rivers

A popular TV and night club personality, Joan Rivers is known for an unsparingly acid tongue.

· · · · ·

"I knew I was an unwanted baby when I saw that my bath toys were a toaster and a radio."

· · · · ·

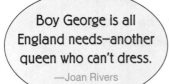

Boy George is all England needs—another queen who can't dress.
—Joan Rivers

"I hate housework. You make the beds, you wash the dishes and six months later you have to start all over again."

· · · · ·

"I told my mother-in-law that my house was her house, and she said, "Get the hell off my property.""

· · · · ·

"My mother could make anybody feel guilty—she used to get letters of apology from people she didn't even know."

Robin Williams

Manic and wildly inventive, Williams may well possess the world's quickest wit.

· · · · ·

"God gave men both a penis and a brain, but unfortunately not enough blood supply to run both at the same time."

· · · · ·

"We had gay burglars the other night. They broke in and rearranged the furniture."

· · · · ·

"If it's the Psychic Network, why do they need a phone number?"

Woody Allen

Allen's intellectual loser persona made the transition from stand-up comedy to successful films.

· · · · · ·

66 My love life is terrible. The last time I was inside a woman was when I visited the Statue of Liberty. 99

· · · · · ·

66 Not only is there no God, but try getting a plumber on weekends. 99

· · · · · ·

66 I am at two with nature. 99

· · · · · ·

It's not that I'm afraid to die. I just don't want to be there when it happens.
—Woody Allen

66 Some guy hit my fender, and I told him, "Be fruitful, and multiply." But not in those words. 99

· · · · · ·

66 I don't want to achieve immortality through my work . . . I want to achieve it through not dying. 99

· · · · · ·

66 I took a speed-reading course and read *War and Peace* in twenty minutes. It's about Russia. 99

Groucho Marx

The raffish roué and verbal gymnast Groucho went from Marx Brothers films to the hit TV show, *You Bet Your Life.*

* * * * *

"From the moment I picked your book up until I laid it down, I was convulsed with laughter. Someday I intend reading it."

* * * * *

"I didn't like the play, but then I saw it under adverse conditions— the curtain was up."

> Outside of a dog, a book is a man's best friend. Inside of a dog, it's too dark to read.
> —Groucho Marx

* * * * *

"I never forget a face, but in your case I'll be glad to make an exception."

* * * * *

"Why, a four-year-old child could understand this report. Run out and find me a four-year-old child. I can't make head nor tail out of it."

* * * * *

"Why should I care about posterity? What's posterity ever done for me?"

Dorothy Parker

One of the Algonquin Hotel "Round Table" wits, Parker wrote short stories and screenplays.

· · · · ·

❝Money cannot buy health, but I'd settle for a diamond-studded wheelchair.❞

· · · · ·

> The two most beautiful words in the English language are "cheque enclosed."
> —Dorothy Parker

❝If you want to know what God thinks of money, just look at the people he gave it to.❞

· · · · ·

❝This is not a novel to be tossed aside lightly. It should be thrown with great force.❞

Erma Bombeck

A newspaper and magazine columnist, Bombeck is adept at finding the humor in everyday life.

· · · · ·

❝Getting out of the hospital is a lot like resigning from a book club. You're not out of it until the computer says you're out of it.❞

· · · · ·

"Do you know what you call those who use towels and never wash them, eat meals and never do the dishes, sit in rooms they never clean, and are entertained till they drop? If you have just answered, "A house guest," you're wrong because I have just described my kids."

· · · · ·

"Making coffee has become the great compromise of the decade. It's the only thing "real" men do that doesn't seem to threaten their masculinity. To women, it's on the same domestic entry level as putting the spring back into the toilet-tissue holder or taking a chicken out of the freezer to thaw."

My kids always perceived the bathroom as a place where you wait it out until all the groceries are unloaded from the car.

—Erma Bombeck

Fred Allen

A literate and absurdist radio comedian, Allen hosted a long-running radio show. His comic feud with Jack Benny was one hallmark of his humor.

· · · · ·

"I always have trouble remembering three things: faces, names, and—I can't remember what the third thing is."

· · · · ·

Happily Un-Married
The Top 15 Answers to "Why Aren't You Married Yet?"

I was hoping to do something meaningful with my life.

What? And spoil my great sex life?

It gives my mother something to live for.

Because I just love hearing this question.

My co-op board doesn't allow spouses.

Why aren't you thin?

Because I think it would take all the spontaneity out of dating.

My fiancé is waiting for his (or her) parole.

What? And lose all the money I've invested in running personal ads?

It didn't seem worth a blood test.

I'm waiting until I get to be your age.

I already have enough laundry to do, thank you.

They just opened a great singles bar on my block.

I'm married to my career, although recently we have been considering a trial separation.

I wouldn't want my parents to drop dead from sheer happiness.

"I like long walks, especially when they are taken by people who annoy me."

· · · · ·

"I can't understand why a person will take a year to write a novel when he can easily buy one for a few dollars."

I'd rather have a full bottle in front of me than a full frontal lobotomy.

—Fred Allen

· · · · ·

"Life, in my estimation, is a biological misadventure that we terminate on the shoulders of six strange men whose only objective is to make a hole in one with you."

· · · · ·

"Television is a medium because anything well done is rare."

· · · · ·

The Best of the Rest
Great one-liners from other famous funny people.

. . . . .

My mom said she learned how to swim. Someone took her out in the lake and threw her off the boat. That's how she learned how to swim.

I said, "Mom, they weren't trying to teach you how to swim." —Paula Poundstone

. . . . .

Ever wonder if illiterate people get the full effect of alphabet soup? —John Mendoza

. . . . .

A study in the *Washington Post* says that women have better verbal skills than men. I just want to say to the authors of that study: Duh. —Conan O'Brien

. . . . .

Who picks your clothes—Stevie Wonder?
—Don Rickles to David Letterman

. . . . .

I WAS A VEGETARIAN UNTIL I STARTED LEANING TOWARDS SUNLIGHT.

—Rita Rudner

THERE IS ONE THING I WOULD BREAK UP OVER AND THAT IS IF SHE CAUGHT ME WITH ANOTHER WOMAN. I WOULDN'T STAND FOR THAT.

—Steve Martin

· · · · ·

Tragedy is when I cut my finger. Comedy is when you fall into an open sewer and die. —Mel Brooks

· · · · ·

I don't like country music, but I don't mean to denigrate those who do. And for the people who like country music, denigrate means "put down." —Bob Newhart

· · · · ·

The trouble with unemployment is that the minute you wake up in the morning you're on the job. —Slappy White

If variety is the spice of life, marriage is the big can of leftover Spam.

—Johnny Carson

· · · · ·

My grandfather always said, "Don't watch your money; watch your health." So one day while I was watching my health, someone stole my money. It was my grandfather. —Jackie Mason

· · · · ·

Any time a person goes into a delicatessen and orders pastrami on white bread, somewhere a Jew dies. —Milton Berle

· · · · ·

When Mel [Brooks] told his Jewish mother he was marrying an Italian girl, she said, "Bring her over. I'll be in the kitchen—with my head in the oven." —Anne Bancroft

· · · · ·

Always be nice to your children because they are the ones who will choose your rest home. —Phyllis Diller

· · · · ·

The problem with the designated driver program, it's not a desirable job. But if you ever get sucked into doing it, have fun with it. At the end of the night, drop them off at the wrong house. —Jeff Foxworthy

· · · · ·

My doctor told me that jogging could add years to my life. He was right—I feel ten years older already. —Milton Berle

· · · · ·

DON'T LET A MAN PUT ANYTHING OVER ON YOU EXCEPT AN UMBRELLA.

—Mae West

· · · · ·

You should always go to other people's funerals; otherwise, they won't come to yours.

—Yogi Berra

Chapter 8

Playoffs

Athletes are so serious, they often don't know how funny they are when they talk about their sport. These quotes will help remind them— and us—that it's all just a game.

Yogi Berra

An all-star catcher with the New York Yankees and then manager of the Yankees and the New York Mets, Berra is well known for his wonderful and deceptively simple use of the English language.

• • • • •

"This is like déjà vu all over again."

• • • • •

"I don't know if it's good for baseball, but it sure beats the hell out of rooming with Phil Rizzuto."

—on being told that Joe DiMaggio was to marry Marilyn Monroe

• • • • •

"If the fans don't come out to the ballpark, you can't stop them."

66 Why buy good luggage? You only use it when you travel. 99

· · · · ·

66 How long have you known me, Jack? And you still don't know how to spell my name. 99

—when he received a check made out to "bearer."

· · · · ·

66 I never blame myself when I'm not hitting. I just blame the bat, and if it keeps up, I change bats. After all, if I know it isn't my fault that I'm not hitting, how can I get mad at myself? 99

Casey Stengel

Manager of the New York Yankees and New York Mets, Stengel's "amazin' " convoluted utterances made him one of baseball's most colorful figures.

· · · · ·

66 All right, everybody line up alphabetically according to your height. 99

· · · · ·

Good pitching will always stop good hitting and vice-versa.
—Casey Stengel

66 You have to have a catcher because if you don't you're likely to have a lot of passed balls. 99

· · · · ·

⟨⟨I was such a dangerous hitter I even got intentional walks in batting practice. ⟩⟩

· · · · · ·

⟨⟨It's wonderful to meet so many friends that I didn't used to like. ⟩⟩

Ralph Kiner

Former Pittsburgh Pirates outfielder Kiner went on to a career in radio and television broadcasting.

· · · · · ·

⟨⟨Hello, everybody. Welcome to Kiner's Corner. This is . . . uh. I'm . . . uh . . . ⟩⟩

· · · · · ·

⟨⟨On Father's Day, we again wish you all happy birthday. ⟩⟩

All of his saves have come in relief appearances.

—Ralph Kiner

· · · · · ·

⟨⟨There's a lot of heredity in that family. ⟩⟩

· · · · · ·

⟨⟨Tony Gwynn was named player of the year for April. ⟩⟩

· · · · · ·

Bob Uecker

A National League catcher whose acting and broadcasting careers far overshadowed his time spent on the field.

· · · · ·

> I knew when my career was over. In 1965 my baseball card came out with no picture.
> —Bob Uecker

❝I signed with the Milwaukee Braves for three-thousand dollars. That bothered my dad at the time because he didn't have that kind of dough. But he eventually scraped it up.❞

· · · · ·

❝The highlight of my career? In '67 with St. Louis, I walked with the bases loaded to drive in the winning run in an intersquad game in spring training.❞

Baseball

I heard the doctors revived a man after being dead for four-and-a-half minutes. When they asked what it was like being dead, he said it was like listening to New York Yankees announcer Phil Rizzuto during a rain delay.

—*Late Night* host David Letterman

· · · · ·

Age is a case of mind over matter. If you don't mind, it don't matter. —Satchel Paige

· · · · ·

FANtastic!
The Top 15 Jeers to throw (with the peanuts!) against the teams we love to hate.

Do you want MY autograph?

Does this team actually practice or do they just show up for the games?

This team should go back to the minors.

You guys would be out of your depth in a parking lot puddle.

I hope this team paid to get in.

This team couldn't beat anything with a stick.

Hurry up and practice, the game has started.

Did this team sign a contract with Palmolive Soap? They're all washed up.

This team couldn't make ice without a recipe.

I've got a better team pulling my sleigh.

Does this team think it's "Ladies Night" out there?

Do you think this team will like this game once they catch on!

Is this team going to play the whole game today?

Bring out the elephants; the clowns are already here.

Maybe this team is all left-handed and they don't know it.

During the 1957 World Series, Yankee catcher Yogi Berra noticed that the Atlanta Braves hitting star Hank Aaron grasped the bat the wrong way. "Turn it around," he said, "so you can see the trademark."

Aaron kept his eye on the pitcher's mound: "Didn't come up here to read. Came up here to hit."

· · · · ·

I HATED TO BAT AGAINST (DON) DRYSDALE. AFTER HE HIT YOU HE'D COME AROUND, LOOK AT THE BRUISE ON YOUR ARM AND SAY, "DO YOU WANT ME TO SIGN IT?"

—Mickey Mantle

· · · · ·

I made a game effort to argue but two things were against me: the umpires and the rules. —Giants manager Leo Durocher

Soccer

I took a whack on my left ankle, but something told me it was my right. —Lee Hendrie

· · · · ·

One accusation you can't throw at me is that I've always done my best. —Alan Shearer

· · · · ·

Interviewer: "Would it be fair to describe you as a volatile player?"

David Beckham: "Well, I can play in the centre, on the right and occasionally on the left side."

· · · · ·

I'D RATHER PLAY IN FRONT OF A FULL HOUSE THAN AN EMPTY CROWD.

—Johnny Giles

· · · · ·

If you don't believe you can win, there is no point in getting out of bed at the end of the day. —Neville Southall

· · · · ·

Without being too harsh on David Beckham, he cost us the match. —Ian Wright

· · · · ·

I'm as happy as I can be—but I have been happier. —Ugo Ehiogu

Football

Football is a mistake. It combines two of the worst things about American life. It is violence punctuated by committee meetings. —George F. Will

· · · · ·

THE ROSE BOWL IS THE ONLY BOWL I'VE EVER SEEN THAT I DIDN'T HAVE TO CLEAN.

—Erma Bombeck

· · · · ·

One player was lost because he broke his nose. How do you go about getting a nose in condition for football?

—Darrell Royal, Texas football coach, on Longhorn injuries resulting from poor physical conditioning

· · · · ·

The reason women don't play football is because eleven of them would never wear the same outfit in public.

—Phyllis Diller

An atheist is a guy who watches a Notre Dame-SMU football game and doesn't care who wins. —Dwight D. Eisenhower

· · · · ·

Are you any relation to your brother, Marv?

—Leon Wood, New Jersey Nets guard, to Steve Albert, Nets TV commentator

· · · · ·

Golf

Golf is a good walk spoiled. —Mark Twain

· · · · ·

Golf is a game whose aim is to hit a very small ball into an even smaller hole, with weapons singularly ill designed for the purpose.

—Winston Churchill

I know I am getting better at golf because I am hitting fewer spectators.

—Gerald Ford

· · · · ·

I had a wonderful experience on the golf course today. I had a hole in nothing. Missed the ball and sank the divot. —Don Adams

· · · · ·

The least thing upset him on the links. He missed short putts because of the uproar of the butterflies in the adjoining meadows. —P. G. Wodehouse

· · · · ·

I HAVE A TIP THAT CAN TAKE FIVE STROKES OFF ANYONE'S GOLF GAME. IT'S CALLED AN ERASER.

—Arnold Palmer

· · · · ·

He has a wonderful short game . . . unfortunately it is off the tee.

—Jimmy Demaret on Bob Hope's golf game

· · · · ·

Columbus went around the world in 1492. That isn't a lot of strokes when you consider the course. —Lee Trevino

· · · · ·

Golf appeals to the idiot in us and the child. Just how childlike golf players become is proven by their frequent inability to count past five. —John Updike

Boxing

[Joe] Frazier is so ugly that he should donate his face to the U.S. Bureau of Wildlife. —Muhammad Ali

I don't like money, actually, but it quiets my nerves.
—Joe Louis

· · · · ·

I fought Sugar [Ray Robinson] so many times, I'm surprised I'm not diabetic. But I did have him off the canvas once . . . when he stepped over my body to leave the ring. —Jake LaMotta

· · · · ·

I'm so fast that last night I turned off the light switch in my hotel room and was in bed before the room was dark.

—Muhammad Ali

It pays me better to knock teeth out than to put them in.

> —Frank Moran, dentist turned prizefighter, when Theodore
> Roosevelt asked him why he changed occupations

Horse Racing

I played a great horse yesterday—it took seven horses to beat him. —Henny Youngman

· · · · ·

They must get to the end and go, "We were just here." What's the point of that?

> —Jerry Seinfeld, on what a horse must think after a race is over

· · · · ·

I hope I break even—I need the money. —Joe E. Lewis

A Gallery of Bronx Cheers
Our Favorite Top 12
McEnroe-style Catcalls

Hey, Mr. Magoo, did you forget your glasses?

They're putting your strike zone on the back of milk cartons.

You couldn't make the right call if you had a phone book.

I've seen potatoes with better eyes.

If you had one more eye you'd be a Cyclops.

If I had a dollar for every good call you've made, I'd be broke!

I thought only horses slept standing up!

If you're just going to watch the game, buy a ticket.

Does your wife let you make decisions at home?

I've gotten better calls from my ex-wife!

Now I know why there's only one "I" in umpire.

I was confused the first time I saw a game too.

A man described as a "sportsman" is generally a bookmaker who takes actresses to nightclubs. —Jimmy Cannon

· · · · ·

THE RACE IS NOT ALWAYS TO THE SWIFT, NOR THE BATTLE TO THE STRONG, BUT THAT'S THE WAY TO BET.

—Damon Runyon

Tennis

It's quite clear that Virginia Wade is thriving on the pressure now that the pressure on her to do well is off.

—Harry Carpenter

The serve was invented so that the net could play.
—Bill Cosby

· · · · ·

When Martina is tense, it helps her relax. —Dan Maskell

· · · · ·

We haven't had any more rain since it stopped raining.

—Harry Carpenter

· · · · ·

Basketball

Nothing there but basketball, a game which won't be fit for people until they set the basket umbilicus-high and return the giraffes to the zoo. —Ogden Nash

· · · · ·

The trouble with referees is that they just don't care which side wins. —Tom Canterbury

· · · · ·

Chemistry is a class you take in high school or college, where you figure out two plus two is ten, or something. —Dennis Rodman

And for the non-sporting breed . . .

Sport—never, ever got involved in sport.
—Winston Churchill on the secret of his longevity

· · · · ·

The only reason I would take up jogging is so I could hear heavy breathing again. —Erma Bombeck

· · · · ·

The first time I see a jogger smiling, I'll consider it. —Joan Rivers

**JOGGING IS FOR PEOPLE WHO AREN'T
INTELLIGENT ENOUGH TO WATCH TELEVISION.**

—Victoria Wood

I did a picture in England
one winter and it was so cold,
I almost got married.

—Shelley Winters

Chapter 9
Film Frolics

Why do we love movies? Is it the pleasure they give us in the viewing or the stars we love to drool over? Either way, here are some quotes to digest before diving into that bucket of popcorn.

It proves what they always say: give the public what they want and they'll come out for it. —Red Skelton, on the funeral of Harry Cohn, a widely disliked movie producer

· · · · ·

I'm an excellent housekeeper. Every time I get a divorce, I keep the house. —Zsa Zsa Gabor

· · · · ·

IN HOLLYWOOD, IF YOU DON'T HAVE HAPPINESS YOU SEND OUT FOR IT.
—Rex Reed

· · · · ·

The Hollywood Cat Fight
Our Top 10 Hollywood Hissy Fits and One-Liners

He is to acting what Liberace was to pumping iron.

—Rex Reed on Sylvester Stallone

I have more talent in my smallest fart than you have in your entire body.

—Walter Matthau to Barbra Streisand

She was divinely, hysterically, insanely malevolent.

—Bette Davis on the silent movie star Theda Bara

You can calculate Zsa Zsa Gabor's age by the rings on her fingers.

—Bob Hope

Dramatic art in her opinion is knowing how to fill a sweater.

—Bette Davis on Jayne Mansfield

A fellow with the inventiveness of Albert Einstein but with the attention span of Daffy Duck.

—Tom Shales on Robin Williams

I didn't know her well, but after watching her in action I didn't want to know her well.

—Joan Crawford on Judy Garland

She turned down the role of Helen Keller because she couldn't remember the lines.

—Joan Rivers on Bo Derek

It's a new low for actresses when you have to wonder what's between her ears instead of her legs.

—Katharine Hepburn on Sharon Stone

His ears made him look like a taxicab with both doors open.

—Howard Hughes on Clark Gable

Give me a couple of years, and I'll make that actress an overnight success. —Samuel Goldwyn

. . . . .

I only put clothes on so that I'm not naked when I go out shopping. —Julia Roberts

. . . . .

I'm so naive about finances. Once when my mother mentioned an amount and I realized I didn't understand, she had to explain: "That's like three Mercedes." Then I understood.

—Brooke Shields

. . . . .

On the one hand, [men] will never experience childbirth. On the other hand, we can open all our own jars. —Bruce Willis

. . . . .

A gentleman is simply a patient wolf. —Lana Turner

. . . . .

WHEN AN ACTOR COMES TO ME AND WANTS TO DISCUSS HIS CHARACTER, I SAY, "IT'S IN THE SCRIPT." IF HE SAYS, "BUT WHAT'S MY MOTIVATION?" I SAY, "YOUR SALARY."

—Alfred Hitchcock

. . . . .

Do you think we should drive a stake through his heart just in case? —Peter Lorre to Vincent Price at Bela Lugosi's funeral

· · · · ·

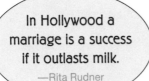

In Hollywood a marriage is a success if it outlasts milk.
—Rita Rudner

What do you want me to do? Stop shooting now and release it as The Five Commandments?
—Cecil B. DeMille, after running over budget on the filming of *The Ten Commandments*

· · · · ·

Joan always cries a lot. Her tear ducts must be close to her bladder. —Bette Davis on Joan Crawford

· · · · ·

Fame means when your computer modem is broken, the repair guy comes out to your house a little faster.
—Sandra Bullock

· · · · ·

I STOPPED BELIEVING IN SANTA CLAUS WHEN I WAS SIX. MOTHER TOOK ME TO SEE HIM IN A DEPARTMENT STORE AND HE ASKED FOR MY AUTOGRAPH.
—Shirley Temple

· · · · ·

Alfred Hitchcock was once detained by an airport customs officer who studied the director's passport's listing his occupation as "Producer." "So what do you produce?" the official asked.

"Gooseflesh!" Hitchcock replied.

· · · · · ·

You can pick out actors by the glazed look that comes into their eyes when the conversation wanders away from themselves. —Michael Wilding

· · · · · ·

For those of you who haven't read the book, it's being published tomorrow. —David Frost

· · · · · ·

CLARK IS THE SORT OF GUY THAT IF YOU SAY, "HIYA, CLARK, HOW ARE YOU?" HE'S STUCK FOR AN ANSWER.

—Ava Gardner on Clark Gable

· · · · · ·

Katharine Hepburn (after making the film *A Bill of Divorcement*): "Mr. Barrymore, I am never going to act with you again."

John Barrymore: "My dear, you still haven't."

· · · · · ·

The scene is dull. Tell him to put more life into his dying.

—Samuel Goldwyn

· · · · ·

IT'S A SCIENTIFIC FACT. FOR EVERY YEAR A PERSON LIVES IN HOLLYWOOD, THEY LOSE TWO POINTS OF THEIR IQ.

—Truman Capote

· · · · ·

He's the type of man who will end up dying in his own arms.

—Mamie Van Doren on Warren Beatty

· · · · ·

I once shook hands with Pat Boone and my whole right side sobered up. —Dean Martin

· · · · ·

THERE ARE GOOD DAYS AND THERE ARE BAD DAYS, AND THIS IS ONE OF THEM.

—Lawrence Welk

· · · · ·

Man, I am a one-eyed, black Jew! That's my handicap!

—Sammy Davis, Jr., asked about his golf handicap

· · · · ·

The Critics Jeer
The Best of the Best of the Zingers

The love story that takes us from time to time into the past is horribly wooden and clichés everywhere lower the tension.

—*New Statesman* on
Casablanca (1942)

This is a pompous, badly acted film, full of absurd anachronisms and inconsistencies.

—Graham Greene, *The Spectator*
on *The Bride of Frankenstein* (1935)

It has dwarfs, music, Technicolor, freak characters and Judy Garland. It can't be expected to have a sense of humor as well, and as for the light touch of fantasy, it weighs like a pound of fruitcake soaking wet.

—*The New Republic* on
The Wizard of Oz (1939)

The old master has turned out another Hitchcock-and-bull story in which the mystery is not so much who done it as who cares.

—*Time* on *Vertigo* (1958)

A bore is starred.

—*Village Voice* review of
A Star Is Born, starring
Barbra Streisand

It's a Frankenstein monster stitched together from leftover parts. It talks. It moves in fits and starts but it has no mind of its own . . . Looking very expensive but spiritually desperate, Part II has the air of a very long, very elaborate revue sketch.

—Vincent Canby on *The Godfather,
Part II* (1974)

The slab is never explained, leaving *2001*, for all its lively visual and mechanical spectacle, a kind of space-*Spartacus* and, more pretentious still, a shaggy God story.

—John Simon, *The New Leader* on
2001: A Space Odyssey (1968)

Every director bites the hand that lays the golden egg.

—Samuel Goldwyn

· · · · ·

An actor's success has the life expectancy of a small boy about to look into a gas tank with a lighted match. —Fred Allen

· · · · ·

She has discovered the secret of perpetual middle age.

—Oscar Levant on Zsa Zsa Gabor

· · · · ·

She ran the whole gamut of emotions from A to B.
—Dorothy Parker on Katharine Hepburn

Each generation has been an education for us in different ways. The first child-with-bloody-nose was rushed to the emergency room. The fifth child-with-bloody-nose was told to go to the yard immediately and stop bleeding on the carpet. —Art Linkletter

· · · · ·

Many a man has fallen in love with a girl in a light so dim he would not have chosen a suit by it. —Maurice Chevalier

· · · · ·

THE PERFECT LOVER IS ONE WHO TURNS INTO A PIZZA AT 4:00 A.M.

—Charles Pierce

HE COULDN'T AD-LIB A FART AFTER A BAKED-BEAN DINNER.

—Johnny Carson on Chevy Chase

· · · · ·

I never mind my wife having the last word. In fact, I'm delighted when she gets to it. —Walter Matthau

· · · · ·

Joan Collins unfortunately can't be with us tonight. She's busy attending the birth of her next husband. —John Parrott

· · · · ·

A verbal contract isn't worth the paper it's written on.

—Samuel Goldwyn

· · · · ·

They say hard work
never hurt anybody, but I
figure why take the chance.

—Ronald Reagan

Chapter 10

Political Badinage

With politicians making statements on key issues facing America today, it's always nice to lighten the moment with some comic relief. The following quotes are some missteps made by our fearless leaders.

George W. Bush

The forty-third president of the United States, Bush is the frequent source of puzzlement and amusement over his use and misuse of the language.

. . . . . .

66 See, in my line of work you got to keep repeating things over and over and over again for the truth to sink in, to kind of catapult the propaganda. 99

. . . . . .

66 Oftentimes, we live in a processed world, you know, people focus on the process and not results. 99

They misunderestimated me.
—George W. Bush

. . . . . .

"It will take time to restore chaos and order."

. . . . .

"They have miscalculated me as a leader."

. . . . .

"I am mindful not only of preserving executive powers for myself, but for predecessors as well."

. . . . .

"I strongly believe what we're doing is the right thing. If I didn't believe it—I'm going to repeat what I said before—I'd pull the troops out, nor if I believed we could win, I would pull the troops out."

. . . . .

> If the Iranians were to have a nuclear weapon, they could proliferate.
> —George W. Bush

"No question that the enemy has tried to spread sectarian violence. They use violence as a tool to do that."

. . . . .

"And so I'm for medical liability at the federal level."

. . . . .

"Because he's hiding." —responding to a reporter who asked why Osama bin Laden had not been caught

66 Natural gas is hemispheric. I like to call it hemispheric in nature because it is a product that we can find in our neighborhoods. 99

· · · · ·

66 If you don't stand for anything, you don't stand for any-thing! If you don't stand for something, you don't stand for anything. 99

· · · · ·

66 We cannot let terrorists and rogue nations hold this nation hostile or hold our allies hostile. 99

Dan Quayle
Vice president under George H. W. Bush, Quayle set the standard for political malapropisms and obfuscation.

· · · · ·

66 One word sums up probably the responsibility of any vice president, and that one word is "to be prepared." 99

Republicans understand the importance of bondage between a mother and child.

—Dan Quayle

· · · · ·

66 Welcome to President Bush, Mrs. Bush, and my fellow astronauts. 99

· · · · ·

"Mars is essentially in the same orbit . . . Mars is somewhat the same distance from the Sun, which is very important. We have seen pictures where there are canals, we believe, and water. If there is water, that means there is oxygen. If oxygen, that means we can breathe."

· · · · ·

"The Holocaust was an obscene period in our nation's history. I mean in this century's history. But we all lived in this century. I didn't live in this century."

· · · · ·

"I believe we are on an irreversible trend toward more freedom and democracy—but that could change."

· · · · ·

"I have made good judgments in the past. I have made good judgments in the future."

· · · · ·

The future will be better tomorrow.
—Dan Quayle

"We're going to have the best-educated American people in the world."

· · · · ·

"People that are really very weird can get into sensitive positions and have a tremendous impact on history."

· · · · ·

Politic Commentary
Our Favorite 10 Wisecracks and Witticisms on America's Leaders

This guy's as bright as an egg timer.

—Chevy Chase on George W. Bush

Hell, if you work for Bill Clinton, you go up and down more times than a whore's nightgown. —White House advisor James Carville

What is his accomplishment? That he's no longer an obnoxious drunk? —Ron Reagan, Jr., on George W. Bush

History buffs probably noted the reunion at a Washington party a few weeks ago of three ex–presidents: Carter, Ford, and Nixon—See No Evil, Hear No Evil, and Evil.

—Robert J. Dole, in a 1983 speech

I am told he no sooner thinks than he talks, which is a miracle not wholly in accord with an educational theory of forming an opinion. —Woodrow Wilson on Theodore Roosevelt

An empty suit that goes to funerals and plays golf.

—Ross Perot on Dan Quayle

Such a little man could not have made so big a depression.

—Norman Thomas on Herbert Hoover

When Al Gore gives a fireside chat, the fire goes out. —Senator Robert Dole

Mr. Wilson bores me with his Fourteen Points; why, God Almighty has only ten.

—Georges Clemenceau on Woodrow Wilson

He can lie out of both sides of his mouth at the same time, and if he ever caught himself telling the truth, he'd lie just to keep his hand in.

—Harry Truman on Richard Nixon

❝We have a firm commitment to NATO, we are a part of NATO. We have a firm commitment to Europe. We are a part of Europe.❞

· · · · ·

❝I am not part of the problem. I am a Republican.❞

Ronald Reagan

The fortieth U.S. president, Reagan made good use of his acting background to use humor as a valuable tool.

· · · · ·

❝The taxpayer—that's someone who works for the federal government but doesn't have to take the civil service examination.❞

· · · · ·

❝I don't know. I've never played a governor.❞
—asked by a reporter in 1966 what kind of governor he would be

· · · · ·

Trees cause
more pollution than
automobiles.
—Ronald Reagan

❝Facts are stupid things.❞ —at the 1988 Republican National Convention, attempting to quote John Adams, who said, "Facts are stubborn things."

· · · · ·

“All the waste in a year from a nuclear power plant can be stored under a desk.”

· · · · ·

“Approximately 80 percent of our air pollution stems from hydrocarbons released by vegetation, so let's not go overboard in setting and enforcing tough emission standards from man-made sources.”

· · · · ·

“How are you, Mr. Mayor? I'm glad to meet you. How are things in your city?” —greeting Samuel Pierce, his secretary of Housing and Urban Development, during a White House reception for mayors

Recession is when your neighbor loses his job. Depression is when you lose yours. And recovery is when Jimmy Carter loses his.

—Ronald Reagan

· · · · ·

“What makes him think a middle-aged actor, who's played with a chimp, could have a future in politics?”

—on Clint Eastwood's bid to become mayor of Carmel

· · · · ·

On Power and Politics

There were four million people in the Colonies and we had Jefferson and Franklin. Now we have over 200 million and the two top guys are Clinton and Dole. What can you draw from this? Darwin was wrong! —Mort Sahl

· · · · ·

Reader, suppose you were an idiot; and suppose you were a member of Congress; but I repeat myself. —Mark Twain

· · · · ·

I would go to the President's wife and apologize, and then leave at once. —Maine Senator Margaret Chase Smith, asked what she would do if she woke up one morning and found herself in the White House.

· · · · ·

The meek shall inherit the earth, but not the mineral rights.
—J. Paul Getty

· · · · ·

THIS IS REALLY EMBARRASSING. I JUST FORGOT OUR STATE GOVERNOR'S NAME, BUT I KNOW THAT YOU WILL HELP ME RECALL HIM.
—Arnold Schwarzenegger

· · · · ·

The one thing I do not want to be called is First Lady. It sounds like a saddle horse. —Jacqueline Kennedy

· · · · ·

The puppies are sleeping on the *Washington Post* and the *New York Times*. It's the first time in history these papers have been used to prevent leaks. —George H. W. Bush

· · · · ·

If life were fair, Dan Quayle would be making a living asking. "Do you want fries with that?" —John Cleese

Things are more like today than they have ever been before.
—Gerald R. Ford

· · · · ·

People are more violently opposed to fur than leather because it's safer to harass rich women than motorcycle gangs.

—source unknown

· · · · ·

I have opinions of my own, strong opinions, but I don't always agree with them. —George H. W. Bush

· · · · ·

What's a man got to do to get in the top fifty?

—Bill Clinton, reacting to a survey of journalists that ranked the Lewinsky scandal as the fifty-third most significant story of the century.

· · · · ·

I have often wanted to drown my troubles, but I can't get my wife to go swimming. —Jimmy Carter

· · · · ·

I WAS PROVIDED WITH ADDITIONAL INPUT THAT WAS RADICALLY DIFFERENT FROM THE TRUTH. I ASSISTED IN FURTHERING THAT VERSION.

—Colonel Oliver North, from his Iran-Contra testimony

· · · · ·

The difference between a misfortune and a calamity is this: If Gladstone fell into the Thames, it would be a misfortune. But if someone dragged him out again, that would be a calamity.

—Benjamin Disraeli

· · · · ·

Confronted at a White House reception by a large, obviously self-satisfied Beacon Hill matron, Coolidge allowed his visitor to pump his arm mechanically while she gushed, "Oh, Mr. President, I'm from Boston."

"Yep," he shot back. "And you'll never get over it."

· · · · ·

IN ARIZONA WE HAVE SO LITTLE WATER THAT THE TREES CHASE THE DOGS.

—Senator Barry Goldwater

· · · · ·

Political Heckles and Hackles
The Best Politico Responses to Nasty Nay-sayers

A political rally heckler to presidential candidate Al Smith: "Go ahead Al. Tell 'em all you know, it won't take long."

Smith replied, "I'll tell 'em all we both know. It won't take any longer."

·

John Randolph, meeting political rival Henry Clay on a narrow sidewalk: "I, sir, do not step aside for a scoundrel."

Clay replied, "I, on the other hand, always do."

·

While delivering a campaign speech one day Theodore Roosevelt was interrupted by a heckler: "I'm a Democrat!" the man shouted. "May I ask the gentleman," Roosevelt replied, quieting the crowd, "why he is a Democrat?"

"My grandfather was a Democrat," the man replied, "my father was a Democrat and I am a Democrat."

"My friend," Roosevelt interjected, "suppose your grandfather had been a jackass and your father was a jackass. What would you then be?"

The heckler replied, "A Republican!"

·

Calvin Coolidge, who was widely known for being miserly with his speech, was approached by a woman who told him, "Mr. President, I bet my friend that I could get you to say three words to me."

Coolidge replied, "You lose."

·

An elderly dowager told to a young Winston Churchill, "There are two things I don't like about you, Mr. Churchill—your politics and your mustache."

Churchill replied, "My dear madam, pray do not disturb yourself. You are not likely to come into contact with either."

·

I think that gay marriage should be between a man and a woman. —Arnold Schwarzenegger

• • • • •

NIXON IS THE KIND OF POLITICIAN WHO WOULD CUT DOWN A REDWOOD TREE, THEN MOUNT THE STUMP FOR A SPEECH ON CONSERVATION.

—Adlai Stevenson

• • • • •

If a politician found he had cannibals among his constituents, he would promise them missionaries for dinner. —H. L. Mencken

• • • • •

At every crisis the Kaiser crumpled. In defeat he fled; in revolution he abdicated; in exile he remarried. —Winston Churchill

• • • • •

When planning what to wear to a costume ball Lady Astor was hosting, Churchill asked her for suggestions.

Her reply: "Why don't you come sober, Mr. Prime Minister."

• • • • •

He would kill his own mother just so that he could use her skin to make a drum to beat his own praises.

—Margot Asquith on Sir Winston Churchill

· · · · ·

Lady Astor once said with exasperation to Churchill, "If you were my husband, I'd put arsenic in your coffee."

Churchill responded, "Madam, if I were your husband, I'd drink it."

· · · · ·

WHEN YOUR BACK'S AGAINST THE WALL IT'S TIME TO TURN ROUND AND FIGHT.

—John Major

· · · · ·

Youth is a wonderful thing. What a crime to waste it on children.

—George Bernard Shaw

Chapter 11

Literary Lampoons

*S*harp satire, rapier wit, magical metaphors.
*. . . they're all part of the wonderful literary
world, as are these stellar quotes about writing
from some of the world's luminaries.*

Fiction writing is great. You can make up almost anything.

—Ivana Trump, on finishing her first novel

· · · · ·

I'm all in favor of keeping dangerous weapons out of the hands of fools. Let's start with typewriters. —Frank Lloyd Wright

· · · · ·

It was a book to kill time for those who like it better dead.

—Rose Macaulay

· · · · ·

A BOOK IS WHAT THEY MAKE A MOVIE OUT OF FOR TELEVISION.

—Leonard Levinson

· · · · ·

I didn't like the play, but then I saw it under adverse conditions— the curtain was up.

—Groucho Marx

Paradise Lost is one of the books which the reader admires and puts down, and forgets to take up again. None ever wished it longer than it is. —Samuel Johnson, on Milton, from *Lives of the Poets*

· · · · ·

There are only two tragedies in life: one is not getting what one wants, and the other is getting it. —Oscar Wilde

· · · · ·

A great many people now reading and writing would be better employed keeping rabbits. —Edith Sitwell

· · · · ·

Nature, not content with denying him the ability to think, has endowed him with the ability to write. —A. E. Housman

· · · · ·

THANK YOU FOR SENDING ME A COPY OF YOUR BOOK—I'LL WASTE NO TIME READING IT.

—Moses Hadas

· · · · ·

Marriage is popular because it combines the maximum of temptation with the maximum of opportunity.

—George Bernard Shaw

This is one of those big, fat paperbacks, intended to while away a monsoon or two, which, if thrown with a good overarm action, will bring a water buffalo to its knees.

—Nancy Banks-Smith (review of M. M. Kaye's *The Far Pavilions*)

· · · · · ·

There was only one catch, and that was Catch-22, which specified that a concern for one's safety in the face of dangers that were real and immediate was the process of a rational mind. Orr was crazy and could be grounded. All he had to do was ask; and as soon as he did, he would no longer be crazy and he would have to fly more missions. Orr would be crazy to fly more missions and sane if he didn't, but if he was sane he had to fly them. If he flew them he was crazy and didn't have to, but if he didn't want to, he was sane and had to.

—Joseph Heller, *Catch-22*

· · · · · ·

Men marry because they are tired; women, because they are curious; both are disappointed. —Oscar Wilde

· · · · · ·

The starting point of this lecturing-trip around the world was Paris, where we had been living a year or two. We sailed for America, and there made certain preparations. This took but little time. Two members of my family elected to go with me. Also a carbuncle. The dictionary says a carbuncle is a kind of jewel. Humor is out of place in a dictionary.

—Mark Twain, *Following the Equator*

· · · · ·

Marriage is like a cage; one sees the birds outside desperate to get in, and those inside desperate to get out. —Montaigne

· · · · ·

A HUSBAND IS WHAT IS LEFT OF THE LOVER AFTER THE NERVE HAS BEEN EXTRACTED.

—Helen Rowland

· · · · ·

By all means marry. If you get a good wife, you'll be happy. If you get a bad one, you'll become a philosopher . . . and that is a good thing for any man. —Socrates

· · · · ·

Don't give a woman advice; one should never give a woman anything she can't wear in the evening. —Oscar Wilde

· · · · ·

The Inspired You
The Top 10 Creative Motivators of the Talented

Think left and think right and think low and think high. Oh, the thinks you can think up if only you try! —Dr. Seuss

Creativity comes from trust. Trust your instincts. And never hope more than you work. —Rita Mae Brown

You should not give anybody the power to decide what is right and wrong in your creativity. —Anaïs Nin

Technique alone is never enough. You have to have passion. Technique alone is just an embroidered potholder. —Raymond Chandler

Curiosity is the key to creativity. —Akio Morita

If you want to work on your art, work on your life. —Anton Chekhov

A long walk and grooming with a well-mannered dog is a Zen experience that leaves you refreshed and in a creative frame of mind. —Dan Koontz

You can't depend on your eyes when your imagination is out of focus. —Mark Twain

When a thing has been said, and said well, have no scruple. Take it and copy it. —Anatole France

Find a need and fill it. —Ruth Stafford Peale

When a society has to resort to the lavatory for its humor, the handwriting is on the wall. —Alan Bennett

· · · · ·

This is no time for making new enemies.
—Voltaire, when asked on his deathbed to renounce the Devil.

· · · · ·

Big sisters are the crab grass in the lawn of life.
—Charles Schulz

All the world's a stage and most of us are desperately unrehearsed. —Sean O'Casey

· · · · ·

I have nothing against undertakers personally. It's just that I wouldn't want one to bury my sister. —Jessica Mitford

· · · · ·

I loathe people who keep dogs. They are cowards who haven't got the guts to bite people themselves. —August Strindberg

· · · · ·

There are times when parenthood seems nothing but feeding the mouth that bites you. —Peter DeVries

· · · · ·

A bride at her second marriage does not wear a veil. She wants to see what she is getting. —Helen Rowland

Many a man owes his success to his first wife and his second wife to his success. —Jim Backus

· · · · ·

I recently read that love is entirely a matter of chemistry. That must be why my wife treats me like toxic waste.

—David Bissonette

· · · · ·

Cats are rather delicate creatures and they are subject to a good many ailments, but I never heard of one who suffered from insomnia. —Joseph Wood Krutch

· · · · ·

THERE ARE ONLY TWO THINGS A CHILD WILL SHARE WILLINGLY; COMMUNICABLE DISEASES AND ITS MOTHER'S AGE.

—Benjamin Spock

· · · · ·

I made my money the old fashioned way. I was very nice to a wealthy relative right before he died. —Malcolm Forbes

· · · · ·

The best measure of a man's honesty isn't his income tax return. It's the zero adjust on his bathroom scale

—Arthur C. Clarke

Bard-olatry
The Top 10 Shakespearean Come-backs

He's a most notable coward, an infinite and endless liar, an hourly promise breaker, the owner of not one good quality.
—All's Well That Ends Well

If thou art changed to aught, 'tis to an ass.
—The Comedy of Errors

Tempt not too much the hatred of my spirit, for I am sick when I do look on thee.
—A Midsummer Night's Dream

Does thy other mouth call me?
—The Tempest

Vile worm, you were overlooked even in thy birth. *—The Merry Wives of Windsor*

I was seeking for a fool when I found you.
—As You Like It

She hath more hair than wit, and more faults than hairs, and more wealth than faults.
—The Two Gentlemen of Verona

Observe him, for the love of mockery.
—Twelfth Night

Female Bastard!
—The Winter's Tale

Beg that thou may have leave to hang thyself.
—The Merchant of Venice

P. G. Wodehouse

The creator of the characters Jeeves and Wooster, Wodehouse (pronounced "Woodhouse") was one of the most admired twentieth-century humorists.

. . . . .

66 There is only one cure for gray hair. It was invented by a Frenchman. It is called the guillotine. 99

. . . . .

66 She fitted into my biggest armchair as if it had been built round her by someone who knew they were wearing armchairs tight about the hips that season. 99

. . . . .

66 For an instance Wilfred Allsop's face lit up, as that of the poet Shelley whom he so closely resembled must have done when realized that "blithe spirit" rhymes with "near it," not that it does, and another ode as good as off the assembly line. 99

. . . . .

66 His first emotion was one of surprise that so much human tonnage could have been assembled at one spot. A cannibal king, beholding them, would have whooped with joy and reached for his knife and fork with the feeling that for once, the catering department had not failed him. 99

. . . . .

❝ Poets, as a class, are business men. Shakespeare describes the poet's eye as rolling in a fine frenzy from heaven to earth, from earth to heaven, and giving to airy nothing a local habitation and a name, but in practice you will find that one corner of that eye is generally glued on the royalty returns. ❞

Ambrose Bierce

Critic and commentator Bierce's *The Devil's Dictionary* was originally called *The Cynic's Word Book*. Its entries deftly lampoon political and social conventions.

· · · · ·

adder: A species of snake. So called from its habit of adding funeral outlays to the other expenses of living.

· · · · ·

painting: The art of protecting flat surfaces from the weather and exposing them to the critic.

· · · · ·

lawsuit: A machine which you go into as a pig and come out of as a sausage.

· · · · ·

love: A temporary insanity curable by marriage.

· · · · ·

egotist (*n.*): A person of low taste, more interested in himself than in me.

· · · · ·

pray: To ask the laws of the universe to be annulled on behalf of a single petitioner confessedly unworthy.

· · · · ·

photograph: A picture painted by the sun without instruction in art.

· · · · ·

sweater (*n.*): Garment worn by child when its mother is feeling chilly.

· · · · ·

Wagner's music is better
than it sounds.

—Mark Twain

Chapter 12
Musical Quirks

Is all music good music? It depends on who is doing the listening (and the composing)!

He has an enormously wide repertory. He can conduct anything, provided it's by Beethoven, Brahms or Wagner. He tried Debussy's La Mer once. It came out as Das Merde.

—anonymous musician on conductor George Szell

. . . . . .

[Richard] Wagner has beautiful moments but bad quarters of an hour. —Gioacchino Rossini

. . . . . .

Dr. Johnson was observed by a musical friend of his to be extremely inattentive at a concert, whilst a celebrated solo player was running up the divisions and subdivisions of notes upon his violin. His friend, to induce him to take greater notice of what was going on, told him how extremely difficult it was.

"Difficult do you call it, Sir?" replied the Doctor; "I wish it were impossible." — John Boswell, *Life of Samuel Johnson*

. . . . . .

Jacques Thibault, the violinist, was once handed an autograph book by a fan while in the greenroom after a concert. "There's not much room on this page," he said. "What shall I write?"

Another violinist overheard the question. "Write your repertoire," he suggested.

· · · · ·

He'd be better off shoveling snow.

—Richard Strauss on Arnold Schoenberg

· · · · ·

NEVER LOOK AT THE TROMBONES; IT ONLY ENCOURAGES THEM.

—Richard Strauss

· · · · ·

I can wait. —Arnold Schoenberg, when told that a soloist would need six fingers to perform his concerto.

· · · · ·

His music used to be original. Now it's aboriginal.

—Sir Ernest Newman on Igor Stravinsky

· · · · ·

If he'd been making shell-cases during the war, it might have been better for music. —Maurice Ravel on Camille Saint-Saens

· · · · ·

IF YOUR LIFEGUARD DUTIES WERE AS GOOD AS YOUR SINGING, A LOT OF PEOPLE WOULD BE DROWNING.

—Simon Cowell, American Idol judge

* * * * *

Someone commented to Rudolf Bing, manager of the Metropolitan Opera, that George Szell is his own worst enemy. "Not while I'm alive, he isn't!" said Bing.

* * * * *

We cannot expect you to be with us all the time, but perhaps you could be good enough to keep in touch now and again. —Sir Thomas Beecham to a musician during a rehearsal

MTV is to music as KFC is to chicken.

—Lewis Black

* * * * *

Already too loud! —Bruno Walter at his first rehearsal with an American orchestra, on seeing the players reaching for their instruments

* * * * *

Artist vs. Artist
7 Snarky Sayings That Made Us Giggle and Gasp

In the match of rhythm and boos, artists can be the most cutting. Of course, most artists have a knack for stringing words together so it's only natural that their taunts would have a sharper sting.

He sang like a hinge.
—Ethel Merman on Cole Porter

[John Lennon] could be a maneuvering swine, which no one ever realized.
—Paul McCartney

Elvis transcends his talent to the point of dispensing with it altogether.
—Greil Marcus on Elvis Presley

She ought to be arrested for loitering in front of an orchestra.
—Bette Midler on Helen Reddy

What a giftless bastard!
—Peter Tchaikovsky on Johannes Brahms

I think Mick Jagger would be astounded and amazed if he realized to how many people he is not a sex symbol but a mother image.
—David Bowie

I love [his] work but I couldn't warm to him even if I was cremated next to him.
—Keith Richards on Chuck Berry

Gadget Guffaws

Here are some slams at instruments and the people who play them.

· · · · ·

Q: How can you tell the difference between bluegrass songs?

A: By their titles.

· · · · ·

Q: Why do some people take an instant aversion to banjo players?

A: It saves time.

· · · · ·

Q: How is lightning like a violist's fingers?

A: Neither one strikes in the same place twice.

· · · · ·

Q: What's the definition of a quarter tone?

A: A harpist tuning unison strings.

· · · · ·

Q: What is the definition of a half step?

A: Two oboes playing in unison.

· · · · ·

Q: Why do bagpipers march when they play?

A: To get away from the noise.

· · · · ·

Q: How do you know when a trombone player is at your door?

A: The doorbell drags.

· · · · ·

Q: Why is the French horn a divine instrument?

A: Because a man blows in it, but only God knows what comes out of it.

· · · · ·

Q: How do you protect a valuable instrument?

A: Hide it in an accordion case.

· · · · ·

Q: What is the definition of an optimist?

A: An accordion player with a pager.

· · · · ·

Q: How do you get two bagpipes to play a perfect unison?

A: Shoot one.

· · · · ·

Q: Why is the banjo player a fiddle player's best friend?

A: Without him, the fiddle would be the most hated instrument on earth.

· · · · ·

Q: How many bass players does it take to change a lightbulb?

A: None. The piano player can do that with his left hand.

· · · · ·

Q: How do you get a cellist to play fortissimo?

A: Write pp, espressivo.

· · · · ·

Q: How do you know if there is a percussionist at the door?

A: The knocking gets slower.

· · · · ·

Q: How do you know when a drum solo's really bad?

A: The bass player notices.

· · · · ·

Q: Why are orchestra intermissions limited to twenty minutes?

A: So you don't have to retrain the cellists.

· · · · ·

Q: How can you tell when there is a drummer at your front door?

A: The knocking gets faster.

· · · · · ·

Q: How do you make a trombone sound like a French horn?

A: Put your hand in the bell and miss a lot of notes.

· · · · · ·

Q: How do you make a violin sound like a viola?

A: Sit in the back and don't play.

· · · · · ·

Q: How do you make a violin sound like a viola?

A: Play in the low register with a lot of wrong notes.

· · · · · ·

Q: How do horn players traditionally greet each other?

A: "Hi. I did that piece in junior high."

Q: What's the difference between a baritone saxophone and a chain saw?

A: The exhaust.

· · · · ·

Q: Why did the bass player get mad at the timpanist?

A: He turned one of the bass's tuning pegs and wouldn't tell the bass player which one.

· · · · ·

Q: What is the difference between the first and last desk of a viola section?

A: Half a measure.

· · · · ·

Q: What is the best recording of the Haydn Trumpet Concerto?

A: Music Minus One.

· · · · ·

Q: What's the difference between trumpet players and government bonds?

A: Government bonds eventually mature and earn money.

· · · · ·

Q: How do you get a guitar player to play softer?

A: Give him a sheet of music.

. . . . .

Q: What do you call two guitarists playing in unison?

A: Counterpoint.

. . . . .

Q: What is the difference between a Wagnerian soprano and an NFL offensive lineman?

A: Stage makeup.

Actual Student Answers to Test Questions About Music

Sherbet composed the Unfinished Symphony.

. . . . .

It is easy to teach anyone to play the maracas. Just grip the neck and shake him in rhythm.

. . . . .

DIATONIC IS A LOW CALORIE SCHWEPPES.

. . . . .

The principal singer of nineteenth-century opera was called pre-Madonna. Gregorian chant has no music, just singers singing the same lines.

· · · · ·

Young scholars have expressed their rapture for the *Bronze Lullaby*, the *Taco Bell Cannon*, Beethoven's *Erotica*, Tchaikovsky's *Cracknutter Suite*, and Gershwin's *Rap City in Blue*.

· · · · ·

Music sung by two people at the same time is called a duel; if they sing without music it is called Acapulco.

· · · · ·

ALL FEMALE PARTS WERE SUNG BY CASTRATI. WE DON'T KNOW EXACTLY WHAT THEY SOUNDED LIKE BECAUSE THERE ARE NO KNOWN DESCENDANTS.

· · · · ·

A virtuoso is a musician with real high morals.

· · · · ·

Probably the most marvelous fugue was the one between the Hatfields and the McCoys.

· · · · ·

THE MAIN TROUBLE WITH A FRENCH HORN
IS THAT IT IS TOO TANGLED UP.

· · · · ·

An interval in music is the distance from one piano to the next.

· · · · ·

The correct way to find the key to a piece
of music is to use a pitchfork.

A harp is a nude piano.

· · · · ·

Agitato is a state of mind when one's finger slips in the middle
of playing a piece.

· · · · ·

Refrain means don't do it. A refrain in music is the part you'd
better not try to sing.

· · · · ·

I KNOW WHAT A SEXTET IS BUT
I'D RATHER NOT SAY.

· · · · ·

Actual Student Answers
to Test Questions
About Music

They Sang What?
Our Favorite Mis-Heard Lyrics

It's a lovely spring day. You're in the car, cruising to one of your
favorite songs, your significant other in the passenger seat
belting it out, when you realize: That's not the right lyric, or is it?
See if you can guess what these misheard lyrics should be.

A birthday with a pot of cheese.
Clue: Eva Cassidy was giving her apologies!

Hope the city voted for you.
Clue: Sandy sang this for Danny Zuko in this musical take on the 1950s greaser era.

Everybody is a wholesale frock.
Clue: It's an Elvis Presley hit.

Got a lot of lucky peanuts.
Clue: Frankie Valli wanted to hang on to this.

Knights speaking Latin.
Clue: White bed linen was the subject of this Moody Blues song!

I'm a pool hall ace.
Clue: The Police ached with each step.

Baking carrot biscuits.
Clue: Randy Bachman paid attention to business.

Just brush my teeth before you leave me.
Clue: Juice Newton thought this was something to do every morning.

Are you going to starve an old friend?
Clue: Simon and Garfunkel went here often.

The girl with colitis goes by.
Clue: The Beatles' Lucy had these.

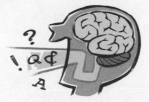

MOST AUTHORITIES AGREE THAT MUSIC OF ANTIQUITY WAS WRITTEN LONG AGO.

· · · · ·

My favorite composer was Opus. Agnus Dei was a woman composer famous for her church music.

· · · · ·

Henry Purcell was a well-known composer few people have ever heard of.

· · · · ·

Contralto is a low sort of music that only ladies sing.

· · · · ·

The main trouble with a French horn is that it is too tangled up.

· · · · ·

WHEN A SINGER SINGS, HE STIRS UP THE AIR AND MAKES IT HIT ANY PASSING EARDRUMS. BUT IF HE IS GOOD, HE KNOWS HOW TO KEEP IT FROM HURTING.

· · · · ·

Actual Student Answers
to Test Questions
About Music

A good orchestra is always ready to play if the conductor steps on the podium.

· · · · ·

An opera is a big song.

· · · · ·

A tuba is much larger than its name.

· · · · ·

Morris dancing is a country survival from times when people were happy.

· · · · ·

Instruments come in many shapes, sizes, and orchestras.

· · · · ·

A trumpet is an instrument when it is not an elephant sound.

· · · · ·

While trombones have tubes, trumpets prefer to wear valves.

· · · · ·

The double bass is also called the bass viol, string bass, and bass fiddle. It has so many names because it is so huge.

· · · · ·

WHEN ELECTRIC CURRENTS GO THROUGH THEM, GUITARS START MAKING SOUNDS. SO WOULD ANYBODY.

· · · · ·

Cymbals are round, metal clangs.

· · · · ·

A bassoon looks like nothing I have ever heard.

· · · · ·

Last month I found out how a clarinet works by taking it apart. I both found out and got in trouble.

· · · · ·

For some reason, they always put a treble clef in front of every line of flute music. You just watch.

· · · · ·

Actual Student Answers
to Test Questions
About Music

Anyone who can read all the instrument notes at the same time gets to be the conductor.

· · · · · ·

Instrumentalist is a many-purpose word for many player-types.

· · · · · ·

The flute is the skinny-high shaped-sounded instrument.

· · · · · ·

THE MOST DANGEROUS PART ABOUT PLAYING CYMBALS IS NEAR THE NOSE.

· · · · · ·

A contra-bassoon is like a bassoon, only more so.

· · · · · ·

France is a country where the money falls apart but you can't tear the toilet paper.

—Billy Wilder

Chapter 13
World Wit

From Dakota to Dubai, and Paris, France to Paris, Texas, humor is humor wherever you go.

He who would eat in Spain must bring his kitchen along.

—German saying

· · · · · ·

Transplanting the ballet to the United States is like trying to raise a palm tree in Dakota. —Lincoln Kirsten

Half of the American people have never read a newspaper. Half never voted for President. One hopes it is the same half.

—Gore Vidal

· · · · · ·

It is quite untrue that British people don't appreciate music. They may not understand it but they absolutely love the noise it makes. —Sir Thomas Beecham

· · · · · ·

The food in Yugoslavia is fine if you like pork tartare.

—Ed Begley, Jr.

· · · · · ·

In America, only the successful writer is important, in France
all writers are important, in England no writer is important,
and in Australia you have to explain what a writer is.

—Geoffrey Cottrell

· · · · ·

Germans are flummoxed by humor, the Swiss have no concept
of fun, the Spanish think there is nothing at all ridiculous
about eating dinner at midnight, and the Italians should
never, ever have been let in on the invention of the motor car.

—Bill Bryson

· · · · ·

There have been many definitions of hell, but for the English
the best definition is that it is the place where the Germans
are the police, the Swedish are the comedians, the Italians
are the defense force, Frenchmen dig the roads, the Belgians
are the pop singers, the Spanish run the railways, the Turks
cook the food, the Irish are the waiters, the Greeks run the
government, and the common language is Dutch.

—David Frost and Anthony Jay

· · · · ·

I LOVE THANKSGIVING TURKEY . . .
IT'S THE ONLY TIME IN LOS ANGELES
THAT YOU SEE NATURAL BREASTS.

—Arnold Schwarzenegger

· · · · ·

WHEN IT'S THREE O'CLOCK IN NEW YORK, IT'S STILL 1938 IN LONDON.

—Bette Midler

· · · · ·

The Irish are a fair people, they never speak well of one another. —Samuel Johnson

· · · · ·

Like an Irishman's obligation, all on the one side, and always yours. —English saying

· · · · ·

The trouble with Ireland is that it's a country full of genius, with absolutely no talent. —Hugh Leonard

· · · · ·

One thing I will say about the Germans, they are always perfectly willing to give somebody's land to somebody else.

—Will Rogers

Because of their cuisine, Germans don't consider farting rude. They'd certainly be out of luck if they did. —P. J. O'Rourke

· · · · ·

I found the pearl of the Orient slightly less exciting than a rainy Sunday evening in Rochester. —S. J. Perelman

· · · · ·

It is after you have lost your teeth that you can afford to buy steaks. —Pierre Renoir

· · · · ·

I FEAR THAT I HAVE NOT GOT MUCH TO SAY ABOUT CANADA, NOT HAVING SEEN MUCH; WHAT I GOT BY GOING TO CANADA WAS A COLD.
—Henry David Thoreau

· · · · ·

The reason there are so many tree-lined boulevards in Paris is so the German Army can march in the shade.
—attributed to General George Patton

· · · · ·

Other people have a nationality. The Irish and the Jews have a psychosis. —Brendan Behan

· · · · ·

Your Country 'Tis of Thee!
The Top 10 Crazy Critiques of America

There is an overwhelming curiosity about all things American, making it very often the butt of a good joke. These fun, foreign views of America are sure to make you smile.

When good Americans die, they go to Paris. When bad Americans die, they go to America. —Oscar Wilde

Americans always try to do the right thing after they've tried everything else. —Winston Churchill

I love Americans, but not when they try to talk French. What a blessing it is that they never try to talk English.
—Saki (H. H. Munro)

Their demeanor is invariably morose, sullen, clownish and repulsive. I should think there is not, on the face of the earth, a people so entirely destitute of humor, vivacity, or the capacity for enjoyment. —Charles Dickens

Never criticize Americans. They have the best taste that money can buy.
—Miles Kingston

The 100% American is 99% idiot.
—George Bernard Shaw

The thing that impresses me most about America is the way parents obey their children.
—King Edward VIII

I found there a country with thirty-two religions and only one sauce.
—Charles-Maurice Talleyrand-Périgord

America is the only nation in history which has miraculously gone directly from barbarism to degeneration without the usual interval of civilization.
—Georges Clemenceau

America is a large, friendly dog in a very small room. Every time it wags its tail, it knocks over a chair. —Arnold Toynbee

No one can be as calculatedly rude as the British, which amazes Americans, who do not understand studied insult and can only offer abuse as a substitute. —Paul Gallico

· · · · ·

The English country gentleman galloping after a fox—the unspeakable in full pursuit of the uneatable. —Oscar Wilde

· · · · ·

The French are sawed-off sissies who eat snails and slugs and cheese that smells like people's feet. Utter cowards who force their own children to drink wine, they gibber like baboons even when you try to speak to them in their own wimpy language. —P. J. O'Rourke

· · · · ·

Part III
Dumbest

Things
Ever Said

· ·

Let's be kind. Just because a person says something dumb, it doesn't mean *they* are dumb. We've all said things we regret. But that doesn't mean we can't enjoy their verbal gaffes. Here are some of the best—or would that be *worst*?

I watch a lot of baseball
on the radio.

—Gerald R. Ford

Chapter 14
Political Howlers

It happens all the time, and it's our good fortune that someone is always around to immortalize the politicians who stumble over their words. Here are some of the oddest.

I've read about foreign policy and studied—I know the number of continents. —George Wallace, 1968 presidential campaign

· · · · ·

Whenever a Republican leaves one side of the aisle and goes to the other, it raises the intelligence quotient of both parties. —Republican Senator Claire Booth Luce, commenting on a certain Republican senator's becoming a Democrat

I can't think of any existing law that's in force that wasn't before.
—George H. W. Bush

· · · · ·

Q: How do you tell Al Gore from the Secret Service Agents?
A: He's the stiff one.

—source unknown

· · · · ·

Nixon's motto was: If two wrongs don't make a right, try three.

—Norman Cousins

· · · · ·

YOU KNOW, IF I WERE A SINGLE MAN, I MIGHT ASK THAT MUMMY OUT. THAT'S A GOOD-LOOKING MUMMY!

—Bill Clinton, looking at the Inca mummy "Juanita"

· · · · ·

For those of you who don't understand Reaganomics, it's based on the principle that the rich and the poor will get the same amount of ice. In Reaganomics, however, the poor get all of theirs in winter. —Morris Udall

· · · · ·

THE DIFFERENCE BETWEEN DEATH AND TAXES IS DEATH DOESN'T GET WORSE EVERY TIME CONGRESS MEETS.

—Will Rogers

· · · · ·

Politics gives guys so much power that they tend to behave badly around women. And I hope I never get into that. —Bill Clinton

· · · · ·

I do not like this word "bomb." It is not a bomb. It is a device that is exploding.

—Jacques le Blanc, French ambassador on nuclear weapons

· · · · ·

I think with a lifetime appointment to the Supreme Court, you can't play, you know, hide the salami, or whatever it's called.

—Democratic Party Chairman Howard Dean, urging President Bush to make public Supreme Court nominee Harriet Miers's White House records, October 5, 2005

· · · · ·

I am not going to give you a number for it because it's not my business to do intelligent work. —Defense Secretary Donald Rumsfeld, asked to estimate the number of Iraqi insurgents while testifying before Congress, February 16, 2005

You can't just let nature run wild.

—Walter Hickel, former governor of Alaska

· · · · ·

He knows nothing and thinks he knows everything. That points clearly to a political career. —George Bernard Shaw

· · · · ·

THEY NEVER OPEN THEIR MOUTHS WITHOUT SUBTRACTING FROM THE SUM OF HUMAN KNOWLEDGE.

—Speaker of the House Thomas Reed of two fellow congressmen

· · · · ·

The Democrats are the party that says government will make you smarter, taller, richer, and remove the crabgrass on your lawn. The Republicans are the party that says government doesn't work and then they get elected and prove it.

—P. J. O'Rourke

· · · · ·

The Democrats seem to be basically nicer people, but they have demonstrated time and again that they have the management skills of celery. —Dave Barry

· · · · ·

He's the only man able to walk under a bed without hitting his head. —Walter Winchell on presidential candidate Thomas E. Dewey

· · · · ·

Don't be so humble, you're not that great. —Golda Meir to Moshe Dayan

· · · · ·

THE WORD LIBERTY IN THE MOUTH OF MR. WEBSTER SOUNDS LIKE THE WORD LOVE IN THE MOUTH OF A COURTESAN.

—Ralph Waldo Emerson

· · · · ·

HE NO PLAY-A THE GAME, HE NO MAKE-A THE RULES.

—Secretary of Agriculture Earl Butz on Pope Pius XII's
attitude toward birth control

· · · · ·

That scoundrel deserves to be kicked to death by a jackass,
and I'm just the one to do it. —A congressional candidate in Texas

· · · · ·

A billion here, a billion there, sooner or later it adds up to real
money. —Everett Dirksen, Congressman

· · · · ·

Solutions are not the answer. —Richard Nixon

· · · · ·

The Right Honorable Gentleman is indebted to his memory
for his jests and to his imagination for his facts.

—Richard Brinsley Sheridan on the Earl of Dundas

· · · · ·

She was happy as the dey was long.

—Lord Norbury on Queen Caroline's affair with the Dey of Algiers

· · · · ·

His intellect is of no more use than a pistol packed in the bottom of a trunk in the robber infested Apennines.
—Prince Albert on his son Edward,
Prince of Wales, later King Edward VII

· · · · ·

Oh, if I could piss the way he speaks!
—Georges Clemenceau on David Lloyd George

· · · · ·

Attila the Hen. —Clement Freud on British Prime Minister Margaret Thatcher

· · · · ·

She sounded like the Book of Revelations read out over a railway station public address system by a headmistress of a certain age wearing calico knickers.
—Clive James on Margaret Thatcher

· · · · ·

THE PRIME MINISTER TELLS US SHE HAS GIVEN THE FRENCH PRESIDENT A PIECE OF HER MIND, NOT A GIFT I WOULD RECEIVE WITH ALACRITY.
—Denis Healy on Margaret Thatcher

· · · · ·

HOW CAN THEY TELL?

—Dorothy Parker, learning of Calvin Coolidge's death

* * * * *

If a traveler were informed that such a man was leader of the House of Commons, he may well begin to comprehend how the Egyptians worshipped an insect.

—Benjamin Disraeli on Prime Minister Lord John Russell

* * * * *

You read what Disraeli had to say. I don't remember what he said. He said something. He's no longer with us. — Bob Dole

* * * * *

I have just read your dispatch about sore-tongued and fatigued horses. Will you pardon me for asking what the horses of your army have done since the battle of Antietam that fatigues anything?

—Abraham Lincoln in a telegram to General George B. McClellan

* * * * *

According to the *L.A. Times*, Attorney General John Ashcroft wants to take "a harder stance" on the death penalty. What's a harder stance on the death penalty? We're already killing the guy. How do you take a harder stance on the death penalty? What, are you going to tickle him first? Give him itching powder? Put a thumbtack on the electric chair? —Jay Leno

* * * * *

If he became convinced tomorrow that coming out for cannibalism would get him the votes he sorely needs, he would begin fattening a missionary in the White House backyard come Wednesday. —H. L. Mencken on Franklin D. Roosevelt

· · · · ·

HE CAN COMPRESS THE MOST WORDS INTO THE SMALLEST IDEAS BETTER THAN ANY MAN I EVER MET.

—Abraham Lincoln, referring to a lawyer

· · · · ·

He turned out to be so many different characters he could have populated all of *War and Peace* and still had a few people left over. —Herbert Mitgang about Lyndon B. Johnson

· · · · ·

He can't help it—he was born with a silver foot in his mouth.
—former Texas governor Ann Richards on George W. Bush

· · · · ·

HE INHERITED SOME GOOD INSTINCTS FROM HIS QUAKER FOREBEARS, BUT BY DILIGENT HARD WORK, HE OVERCAME THEM.

—James Reston on Richard Nixon

· · · · ·

Asking an incumbent member of Congress to vote for term limits is a bit like asking a chicken to vote for Colonel Sanders.

—Bob Inglis

· · · · ·

Bush is smart. I don't think that Bush will ever be impeached, 'cause unlike Clinton, Reagan, or even his father, George W. is immune from scandal. Because, if George W. testifies that he had no idea what was going on, wouldn't you believe him? —Jay Leno

Thanks for the poncho.

—Bill Clinton, when presented with the Romanian tricolor flag during a visit to that country

· · · · ·

It has not worked. No one can say it has worked, so I decided we're either going to do what we said we're going to do with the UN, or we're going to do something else.

—Bill Clinton, on the UN operation in Bosnia

· · · · ·

How Dumb Is He?
The Top Twelve
Stupidity Descriptions

When the next election comes around, you'll be ready with these
phrases to characterize the leader you love to hate.

He's a prime candidate for natural deselection.

•

The world's foremost collector of ignorance.

•

Like a pair of children's scissors, bright and
colorful, but not too sharp.

•

A couple of blocks behind the parade.

•

If stupid were a talent he'd be consider gifted.

•

Too dumb to pull his head in before he shuts the window.

•

When a thought crosses his mind, it's a long and lonely journey.

•

If his brains were dynamite, he couldn't blow his hat off!

•

An experiment in Artificial Stupidity.

•

About as necessary as dinosaur repellant.

•

Forgot to pay his brain bill.

•

If you stand close enough to him you can hear the ocean.

•

As I was telling my husb— . . . As I was telling President Bush . . .
—Condoleezza Rice, unmarried national security advisor

· · · · ·

It's not true the Congressman was sleeping during the debate.
He was just taking a few moments for deep reflection.
—aide to Rep. Martin Hoke, who was spotted on the House of
Representatives floor with eyes closed during a debate

· · · · ·

I THINK WE'RE ON THE ROAD TO COMING UP WITH ANSWERS THAT I DON'T THINK ANY OF US IN TOTAL FEEL WE HAVE THE ANSWERS TO.
—Kim Anderson, mayor of Naples, Florida

· · · · ·

A proof is a proof. What kind of a proof? It's a proof. A proof
is a proof. And when you have a good proof, it's because it's
proven. —Jean Chrétien

· · · · ·

You reporters should have printed what he meant, not what
he said. —Earl Bush, aide to Chicago mayor Richard Daley

· · · · ·

Give Bill a second term, and Al Gore and I will be turned
loose to do what we really want to do.
—Hillary Clinton, speaking at a 1996 Democratic fund-raiser

The Internet is a gateway to get on the Net.

—Bob Dole, former senator

· · · · · ·

We've got a strong candidate. I'm trying to think of his name.
—Senator Christopher Dodd

Things are more like they are now than they ever were before.

—Dwight D. Eisenhower

· · · · · ·

If the King's English was good enough for Jesus, it's good enough for me! —Ma Ferguson, former governor of Texas

· · · · · ·

Beginning in February 1976, your assistance benefits will be discontinued. Reason: It has been reported to our office that you expired on January 1, 1976.

—from a letter by Illinois Department of Public Aid

· · · · · ·

China is a big country, inhabited by many Chinese.

—Charles de Gaulle, former president of France

· · · · · ·

Poultry waste . . . is something that continues to threaten our country. —Tom Daschle, former senator from South Dakota

· · · · · ·

You always write it's bombing, bombing, bombing. It's not bombing, it's air support. —David Opfer, U.S. Air Force colonel, criticizing reporters' coverage of the Vietnam War

. . . . .

I tell you, that Michael Jackson is unbelievable, isn't he? Three plays in twenty seconds! —Al Gore, commenting on basketball star Michael Jordan

A zebra cannot change its spots.
—Al Gore

. . . . .

People who like this sort of thing will find this the sort of thing they like. —Abraham Lincoln

. . . . .

We do not have censorship. What we have is a limitation on what newspapers can report.

—Louis Nel, deputy foreign minister from South Africa

. . . . .

I'm not indecisive. Am I indecisive?

—Jim Scheibel, mayor of St. Paul, Minnesota

. . . . .

It's not easy getting up here and saying nothing. It takes a lot of preparation. —Barry Toiv, White House spokesman

. . . . .

I'm not going to have some reporters pawing through our papers. We are the president. —Hillary Clinton

· · · · ·

IT ISN'T POLLUTION THAT'S HARMING THE ENVIRONMENT. IT'S THE IMPURITIES IN OUR AIR AND WATER THAT ARE DOING IT.

—Dan Quayle

· · · · ·

During my service in the United States Congress, I took the initiative in creating the Internet. —Al Gore

· · · · ·

We don't necessarily discriminate. We simply exclude certain types of people. —Colonel Gerald Wellman, ROTC instructor

· · · · ·

If we don't succeed, we run the risk of failure. —Bill Clinton

· · · · ·

In every country the Communists have taken over, the first thing they do is outlaw cockfighting. —John Monks, state representative from Oklahoma, arguing against a bill to outlaw cockfighting in his state

· · · · ·

We are ready for an unforeseen event that may or may not occur. —Al Gore

· · · · ·

My fellow Americans, I've signed legislation that will outlaw Russia forever. We begin bombing in five minutes. —Ronald Reagan, unaware a radio microphone was on

· · · · ·

Attaboy, Senator! Atta—uh, girl . . . person . . . what are you anyway? —Senator Jesse Helms addressing a female colleague

· · · · ·

Traditionally, most of Australia's imports come from overseas.
—Keppel Enderbery, former Australian cabinet minister

· · · · ·

I FAVOR THE CIVIL RIGHTS ACT OF 1964 AND IT MUST BE ENFORCED AT GUNPOINT IF NECESSARY.
—Ronald Reagan

· · · · ·

I would have voted against the Civil Rights Act of 1964.
—Ronald Reagan

· · · · ·

Your food stamps will be stopped effective March 1992 because we received notice that you passed away. May God bless you. You may reapply if there is a change in your circumstances. —Department of Social Services, Greenville, South Carolina

· · · · ·

There is a mandate to impose a voluntary return to traditional values. —Ronald Reagan

· · · · ·

I don't intend for this to take on a political tone. I'm just here for the drugs. —Nancy Reagan, speaking at an anti-drug rally

· · · · ·

If somebody has a bad heart, they can plug this jack in at night as they go to bed and it will monitor their heart throughout the night. And the next morning, when they wake up dead, there'll be a record. —Mark S. Fowler, FCC chairman

· · · · ·

HAVING COMMITTED POLITICAL SUICIDE, THE CONSERVATIVE PARTY IS NOW LIVING TO REGRET IT.

—Chris Patten, British politician

· · · · ·

Sure, [pesticides] are going to kill a lot of people, but they may be dying of something else anyway.

—Othal Brand, member of Texas pesticide review board

· · · · ·

We have every mixture you can think of. I have a black, I have a woman, two Jews, and a cripple.

—James Watt, Secretary of the Interior, on the diversity of his staff

· · · · ·

Honest businessmen should be protected from the unscrupulous consumer. —Lester Maddox, governor of Georgia, arguing against the creation of a state consumer protection agency

· · · · ·

He's trying to take the decision out of the hands of twelve honest men and give it to congressmen! —Charles Vanik, Ohio congressman, reacting to former Vice President Agnew's request to have his corruption case tried by the House of Representatives

In the early sixties, we were strong, we were virulent . . .
—John Connally, Secretary of the Treasury under Richard Nixon

· · · · ·

These people were highly susceptible to homicide. We know that because they were killed. —Paul Blackman, research coordinator at the National Rifle Association, criticizing a study showing that guns in the home are found to increase risk of death

· · · · ·

The streets are safe in Philadelphia; it's only the people who make them unsafe. —Frank Rizzo, former mayor of Philadelphia

· · · · ·

I've always thought that underpopulated countries in Africa are vastly underpolluted. —Lawrence Summers, chief economist of the World Bank, explaining why we should export toxic wastes to Third World countries

· · · · ·

I can't believe that we are going to let a majority of the people decide what is best for this state.
—John Travis, representative from Louisiana

· · · · ·

The Knights of Peter Claver is a large Catholic organization.
—Wilfred Pierre, representative from Louisiana

· · · · ·

I'm a large Catholic, and I don't belong to it.

—Juba Diez, representative from Louisiana

· · · · ·

I DON'T KNOW ANYONE HERE THAT'S BEEN KILLED WITH A HANDGUN.

—Rep. Avery Alexander, D-New Orleans, to the House of Representatives

· · · · ·

This amendment does more damage than it does harm.

—Cynthia Willard-Lewis, representative from Louisiana

· · · · ·

I think we have passed something that we didn't want to do.

—Chuck McMains, representative from Louisiana

· · · · ·

Y'all are hurting my tender ears. I would appreciate it if y'all would scream one at a time.

—John Alario, House Speaker from Louisiana

· · · · ·

I am honored today to begin my first term as the governor of Baltimore—that is, Maryland. —William Schaefer

· · · · ·

I now have absolute proof that smoking even one marijuana cigarette is equal in brain damage to being on Bikini Island during an H-bomb blast. —Ronald Reagan

· · · · ·

NOW WE ARE TRYING TO GET UNEMPLOYMENT TO GO UP, AND I THINK WE'RE GOING TO SUCCEED.
—Ronald Reagan

· · · · ·

The President has kept all of the promises he intended to keep.
—Clinton White House aide George Stephanopoulos

· · · · ·

If you let that sort of thing go on, your bread and butter will be cut right out from under your feet.
—Ernest Bevin, British foreign minister

· · · · ·

I'm not against the blacks, and a lot of the good blacks will attest to that. —Evan Mecham, governor of Arizona

· · · · ·

I haven't committed a crime. What I did was fail to comply with the law. —David Dinkins, mayor of New York City

· · · · ·

Nixon has been sitting in the White House while George McGovern has been exposing himself to the people of the United States. —Frank Licht, governor of Rhode Island

They gave me a book of checks. They didn't ask for any deposits.
—Joe Early, Massachusetts congressman, on the House bank scandal

He [President Bush] didn't say that. He was reading what was given to him in a speech. —Richard Darman, Office of Management and Budget director

When more and more people are thrown out of work, unemployment results. —Calvin Coolidge

I didn't accept it. I received it.
—Richard Allen, Reagan White House national security advisor, explaining gifts given by two Japanese journalists after he helped arrange a private interview with Nancy Reagan

I was a pilot flying an airplane and it just so happened that where I was flying made what I was doing spying.
—Francis Gary Power, reconnaissance pilot captured by the Soviets

I REGRET TO SAY THAT WE OF THE FBI ARE POWERLESS TO ACT IN CASES OF ORAL-GENITAL INTIMACY, UNLESS IT HAS IN SOME WAY OBSTRUCTED INTERSTATE COMMERCE.

—J. Edgar Hoover, FBI director

· · · · · ·

In the words of George Bernard Shaw, "Two roads diverged in a wood, and I—I took the one less traveled by." —Indiana governor Evan Bayh, misquoting and misidentifying Robert Frost, in a speech calling for educational excellence given at a meeting of the Indiana Educational Committee

· · · · · ·

The Maastricht Treaty . . . has been dealt, at least temporarily, a fatal blow. —Des O'Malley, Irish government minister

· · · · · ·

I'm running for president of the United States because I believe that—with strong leadership—America's days will always lie ahead of us. Just as they lie ahead of us now.

—Bob Dole

· · · · · ·

Those who survived the San Francisco earthquake said, "Thank God, I'm still alive." But of course, those who died— their lives will never be the same again.

—Barbara Boxer, representative from California

· · · · · ·

Hall of Shame

Here are three former prominent leaders in the doghouse.

GEORGE W. BUSH, the forty-third president of the United States, has become infamous for his ability to spend a lot of time saying very little. The following quotes are among his hundreds of brilliantly dumb statements.

> **It will take time to restore chaos and order.**
>
> •
>
> **If you're sick and tired of the politics of cynicism and polls and principles, come and join this campaign.**

MARION BARRY, former mayor of Washington, D.C., is famous for his ability to mix up his words. Talk about mangling the language!

> **Outside of the killings, Washington has one of the lowest crime rates in the country.**
>
> •
>
> **What we have here is an egregemous miscarriagement of taxitude.**
>
> •
>
> **I promise you a police car on every sidewalk.**

DAN QUAYLE, vice president under President George H. W. Bush, is perhaps better known for his verbal blunders than for his politics. Let us pause and remember the good ol' days of the first Bush administration, when men were men and a potato was a potatoe.

> **I stand by all my misstatements.**
>
> •
>
> **What a waste it is to lose one's mind. Or not to have a mind is being very wasteful. How true that is.**

Capital punishment is our society's recognition of the sanctity of human life. —Orrin G. Hatch, senator from Utah

· · · · ·

DEMOCRACY USED TO BE A GOOD THING, BUT NOW IT HAS GOTTEN INTO THE WRONG HANDS.
—Jesse Helms, senator from North Carolina

· · · · ·

But we are not about to send American boys nine or ten thousand miles away from home to do what Asian boys ought to be doing for themselves. —Lyndon B. Johnson

· · · · ·

The United States has much to offer the third world war.
—Ronald Reagan, repeating this mistake nine times in the same address

· · · · ·

He was a man of great statue.
—Thomas Menino, former mayor of Boston

· · · · ·

Sure, I look like a white man. But my heart is as black as anyone's here.
—George Wallace, governor of Alabama, to a predominantly African-American audience

The best cure for insomnia is to get a lot of sleep.
—Senator S. I. Hayakawa

· · · · ·

Bill Weld will not tiptoe around Washington, D.C., on bended knee. —William Weld, Massachusetts governor

· · · · ·

The United States will work toward the elimination of human rights. —in a pledge to El Salvador

I would not have married Dan Quayle had I not thought he was an equal to me. —Marilyn Quayle

· · · · ·

The Jews and Arabs should settle their dispute in the true spirit of Christian charity. —Alexander Wiley, senator from Wisconsin

· · · · ·

This is unparalyzed in the state's history.

—Gib Lewis, Texas Speaker of the House

· · · · ·

The police are not here to create disorder, they're here to preserve disorder. —Richard Daley, former mayor of Chicago

· · · · ·

We are not without accomplishment. We have managed to distribute poverty equally.

—Nguyen Co Thach, Vietnamese foreign minister

· · · · ·

We are getting into semantics again. If we use words, there is a very grave danger they will be misinterpreted. —H. R. Haldeman

. . . . .

I understand it's a nice lifestyle. I love golf, and I understand they have a lot of nice golf courses. —Chic Hecht, senator from Nevada, on why he should be appointed ambassador to the Bahamas

. . . . .

Justice is incidental to law and order. —J. Edgar Hoover

. . . . .

We were at war. They were an endangered species.
—Howard Coble, representative from North Carolina, insisting that the internment of Japanese-Americans during World War II was for their own protection

. . . . .

[OSAMA BIN LADEN] IS EITHER ALIVE AND WELL, OR ALIVE AND NOT WELL, OR NOT ALIVE.
—Donald Rumsfeld, secretary of defense

. . . . .

Everybody was saying we must have more leisure. Now they are complaining they are unemployed.
—Prince Philip, during the 1981 recession

. . . . .

If a cricketer suddenly decided to go into a school and batter a lot of people to death with a cricket bat—which he could do very easily—I mean, are you going to ban cricket bats?
—Prince Philip, reacting to proposals to ban firearms

· · · · ·

IF IT HAS GOT FOUR LEGS AND ISN'T A CHAIR, IF IT HAS GOT TWO WINGS AND ISN'T A PLANE, AND IF IT SWIMS AND ISN'T A SUBMARINE, THE CANTONESE WILL EAT IT.
—Prince Philip

· · · · ·

You are a woman, aren't you?
—Prince Philip, in Kenya, 1984, after accepting a gift from a native woman

· · · · ·

One of our nation's greatest leaders was Hubert Horatio Hornblower . . . —Jimmy Carter, referring to Vice President Hubert Horatio Humphrey in Carter's 1978 presidential nomination acceptance speech

· · · · ·

George Bush doesn't have the manhood to apologize.
—Walter Mondale

· · · · ·

WELL, ON THE MANHOOD THING, I'LL PUT MINE UP AGAINST HIS ANY TIME.

—George H. W. Bush

The exports include thumbscrews and cattle prods, just routine items for the police. —a Commerce Department spokesman on allowing the export of various products

· · · · ·

After finding no qualified candidates for the position of principal, the school department is extremely pleased to announce the appointment of David Steele to the post.

—Philip Streifer, superintendent of schools, Barrington, Rhode Island

· · · · ·

Wait a minute! I'm not interested in agriculture. I want the military stuff.

—William Scott, senator from Virginia, when he was told about missile silos

President Carter speaks loudly and carries a fly spotter, a fly swasher—it's been a long day. —Gerald Ford

. . . . .

It depends on your definition of "asleep." They were not stretched out. They had their eyes closed. They were seated at their desks with their heads in a nodding position.
—John Hogan, plant official, responding to a charge that two nuclear plant operators were sleeping on the job

. . . . .

I am a jelly doughnut. —English translation of John F. Kennedy's "Ich bin ein berliner" line at the Berlin Wall ["I am a Berliner" is, incorrect German, "Ich bin berliner"—the *ein* makes the sentence refer to a berliner, a type of pastry]

. . . . .

WITHOUT CENSORSHIP, THINGS CAN GET TERRIBLY CONFUSED IN THE PUBLIC MIND.
—General William Westmoreland

. . . . .

The chances of Amsterdam becoming a car-free city are as big as the chances of me getting involved in a relationship. If it might ever come to that, I'll calculate what it is going to cost me and I will not go through with it after all.
—a Dutch politician reacting to a question about whether autos should be banned from the center of the city

. . . . .

We must rise to higher and higher platitudes together.

—Richard J. Daley, mayor of Chicago

·····

IF I SEEM UNDULY CLEAR TO YOU, YOU MUST HAVE MISUNDERSTOOD WHAT I SAID.

—Alan Greenspan, Federal Reserve chairman

·····

Now, like, I'm President. It would be pretty hard for some drug guy to come into the White House and start offering it up, you know? . . . I bet if they did, I hope I would say, "Hey, get lost. We don't want any of that." —George H. W. Bush

FOR SEVEN AND A HALF YEARS I'VE WORKED ALONGSIDE PRESIDENT REAGAN. WE'VE HAD TRIUMPHS. MADE SOME MISTAKES. WE'VE HAD SOME SEX . . . UH . . . SETBACKS.

—George H. W. Bush

·····

The caribou love it [the Alaska pipeline]. They rub against it and they have babies. There are more caribou in Alaska than you can shake a stick at. —George H. W. Bush

·····

I don't care what the tape says. I didn't say it.

—Ray Malavasi, St. Louis Rams coach

Chapter 15
Let the Games Begin

As the last notes of the national anthem fade away, you take your seat to watch another feat of athletic prowess. This selection of quotes is sure to get your blood pumping.

Baseball

Any pitcher who throws at a batter and deliberately tries to hit him is a Communist. —Alvin Dark, New York Giants infielder

. . . . .

Well, I see in the game in Minnesota that Terry Felton has relieved himself on the mound in the second inning.
   —Fred White, Kansas City Royals sportscaster, reading a wire-service summary that erroneously named the same starter and relief pitcher for the Minnesota Twins

. . . . .

Even Napoleon had his Watergate.
                —Danny Ozark, Philadelphia Phillies manager

. . . . .

FOLKS, THIS IS PERFECT WEATHER FOR TODAY'S GAME. NOT A BREATH OF AIR.

—Curt Gowdy, sports commentator

· · · · ·

If Jesus were on the field, he'd be pitching inside and breaking up double plays. He'd be high-fiving the other guys.

—Tim Burke, Montreal Expos pitcher

· · · · ·

All I said was that the trades were stupid and dumb, and they took that and blew it all out of proportion.

—Ron Davis, Minnesota Twins pitcher

· · · · ·

I am throwing twice as hard as I ever did. It's just not getting there as fast. —Lefty Gomez, New York Yankees pitcher

· · · · ·

I WAS THE WORST HITTER EVER. I NEVER EVEN BROKE A BAT UNTIL LAST YEAR WHEN I WAS BACKING OUT OF THE GARAGE.

—Lefty Gomez

· · · · ·

I prefer fast food.

—infielder Rocky Bridges, when asked why he would not eat snails

The doctors X-rayed my head and found nothing.

—Dizzy Dean, National League pitcher, after being hit on the
head by a ball in the 1934 World Series

*   *   *   *   *

Her name's Mrs. Coleman. She likes me.

—Choo Choo Coleman, New York Mets catcher, when asked
by Ralph Kiner for his wife's name and what she was like

*   *   *   *   *

I dunno. I never smoked any Astroturf. —Tug McGraw, National
League pitcher, when asked whether he preferred grass or Astroturf

*   *   *   *   *

Always root for the winner. That way you won't be disappointed.

—Tug McGraw

*   *   *   *   *

I told [General Manager] Roland
Hemond to go out and get me a
big-name pitcher. He said, "Dave
Wehrmeister's got eleven letters. Is
that a big enough name for you?"

—Eddie Eichorn, Chicago White Sox owner

*   *   *   *   *

RAISE THE URINALS.

—Darrel Chaney, Atlanta Braves infielder,
on how to keep the Braves on their toes

·····

I'm a four-wheel-drive-pickup type of guy. So is my wife.

—Mike Greenwell, Boston Red Sox outfielder

·····

They shouldn't throw at me. I'm the father of five or six kids.

—Tito Fuentes, National League infielder

There is one word in America that says it all, and that word is, "You never know."

—Joaquin Andujar, National League pitcher

·····

That's why I don't talk. Because I talk too much.

—Joaquin Andujar

·····

Sometimes they write what I say and not what I mean.

—Pedro Guerrero, National League infielder/outfielder

·····

WELL, THAT KIND OF PUTS A DAMPER
ON EVEN A YANKEE WIN.

—Phil Rizzuto, Yankees broadcaster, upon hearing that Pope Paul had died

·····

I LOST IT IN THE SUN!

—Billy Loes, Brooklyn Dodgers pitcher, after fumbling a grounder

· · · · ·

I want all the kids to do what I do, to look up to me. I want all the kids to copulate me.

—Andre Dawson, Chicago Cubs outfielder, on being a role model

· · · · ·

IT WOULD TAKE SOME OF THE LUST OFF THE ALL-STAR GAME.

—Pete Rose, Cincinnati Reds infielder/outfielder,
asked about inter-league play

· · · · ·

It could permanently hurt a batter for a long time.

—Pete Rose, describing a brushback pitch

· · · · ·

Me and George and Billy are two of a kind.

—Mickey Rivers, Texas Rangers outfielder, on his relationship with
Yankees owner George Steinbrenner and manager Billy Martin

· · · · ·

His [Dwight Gooden's] reputation preceded him before he got here. —Don Mattingly, New York Yankees infielder

· · · · ·

Football

If you can't make the putts and can't get the man in from second in the bottom of the ninth, you're not going to win enough football games in this league, and that's the problem we had today. —Sam Rutigliano, Cleveland Browns coach

· · · · ·

He fakes a bluff. —Ron Fairly, New York Giants commentator

· · · · ·

Men, I want you just thinking of one word all season. One word and one word only: Super Bowl.
—Bill Peterson, Florida State football coach

Nobody in football should be called a genius. A genius is a guy like Norman Einstein.
—Joe Theismann, player/commentator

· · · · ·

He [his coach] treats us like men. He lets us wear earrings.
—Torrin Polk, University of Houston receiver

· · · · ·

I MAY BE DUMB, BUT I'M NOT STUPID.
—Terry Bradshaw, player/announcer

· · · · ·

I'm not allowed to comment on lousy officiating.
—Jim Finks, New Orleans Saints general manager

I want to rush for 1,000 or 1,500 yards, whichever comes first.

— George Rogers, New Orleans Saint running back

Basketball

. . . and referee Richie Powers called the loose bowel foul on Johnson.

— Frank Herzog, Washington sports announcer

· · · · ·

I've never had major knee surgery on any other part of my body.

— Winston Bennett, University of Kentucky basketball forward

· · · · ·

Left hand, right hand, it doesn't matter. I'm amphibious.

— Charles Shackleford, North Carolina State player

· · · · ·

I've won at every level, except college and pro.

— Shaquille O'Neal, Los Angeles Lakers player

· · · · ·

We're going to turn this team around 360 degrees.

— Jason Kidd, New Jersey Nets player

· · · · ·

A LOT IS SAID ABOUT DEFENSE, BUT AT THE END OF THE GAME, THE TEAM WITH THE MOST POINTS WINS—THE OTHER TEAM LOSES.

—Isaiah Thomas

· · · · · ·

It's almost like we have ESPN. —Magic Johnson, Los Angeles Lakers player, referring to how well teammate James Worthy and he play together

· · · · · ·

I can't really remember the names of the clubs that we went to. —Shaquille O'Neal, Los Angeles Lakers player, on whether he had visited the Parthenon during a trip to Greece

· · · · · ·

My sister's expecting a baby, and I don't know if I'm going to be an uncle or an aunt. —Chuck Nevitt, North Carolina State basketball player, on why he appeared nervous at practice

· · · · · ·

Hall of Shame

Here are four sports legends lining up for their turn at bat.

Few sports figures—and indeed, few figures in any endeavor—have achieved the verbal notoriety of LAWRENCE "YOGI" BERRA, former catcher of the New York Yankees. Herewith, a smattering of his indescribable utterances:

Slump? I ain't in no slump.
I just ain't hitting.

•

I always thought that record would stand until it was broken.

•

You better cut the pizza in four pieces because I'm not hungry enough to eat six.

RALPH KINER, Pittsburgh Pirates Hall of Fame slugger, has been a radio and television broadcast voice of the New York Mets since 1962. May his legacy continue with lines like these:

Solo homers usually come with no one on base.

•

All of his saves have come in relief appearances.

•

Today is Father's Day, so to all you fathers out there, we'd just like to say, Happy Birthday!

CHARLES "CASEY" STENGEL, Yankees Hall of Fame manager, was another master of obfuscation:

If anyone wants me, tell them I'm being embalmed.

•

All right, everybody line up alphabetically according to your height.

•

If we're going to win the pennant, we've got to start thinking we're not as good as we think we are.

JERRY COLEMAN was an infielder for the Yankees (what is it about the Bronx Bombers that turned out such a raft of funny speakers?), and manager of the San Diego Padres. After playing, he made his mark as a radio and TV broadcaster, where his malapropisms, non-sequiturs, and other goofs became legendary.

At the end, excitement maintained its hysteria.

•

I've made a couple of mistakes I'd like to do over.

•

A day without newspapers is like walking around without your pants on.

I'LL ALWAYS BE NUMBER 1 TO MYSELF.

—Moses Malone, Philadelphia 76ers player

· · · · ·

Tom. —Tom Nissalke, coach of the Houston Rockets, when asked how he pronounced his name

· · · · ·

I'm going to graduate on time, no matter how long it takes.

—unnamed basketball senior, University of Pittsburgh

Soccer

If we played like that every week, we wouldn't be so inconsistent. —Bryan Robson

· · · · ·

And Arsenal now have plenty of time to dictate the last few seconds. —Peter Jones

· · · · ·

It's now 1–1, an exact reversal of the score on Saturday.

—Radio 5 Live

· · · · ·

... and some 500 Italians make the trip, in a crowd of only 400.

—David Smith

· · · · ·

Strangely, in slow-motion replay, the ball seemed to hang in the air for even longer. —David Acfield

· · · · ·

What I said to them at halftime would be unprintable on the radio.

—Gerry Francis

Newcastle, of course, unbeaten in their last five wins. —Brian Moore

· · · · ·

If there weren't such a thing as football, we'd all be frustrated footballers. —Mick Lyons

· · · · ·

He's one of those footballers whose brains are in his head.

—Derek Johnstone

· · · · ·

THE CROWD THINKS THAT TODD HANDLED THE BALL–THEY MUST HAVE SEEN SOMETHING THAT NOBODY ELSE DID.

—Barry Davies

· · · · ·

WELL, EITHER SIDE COULD WIN IT, OR IT COULD BE A DRAW.

—Ron Atkinson, soccer player

· · · · ·

Both of the Villa scorers—Withe and Mortimer—were born in Liverpool, as was the Villa manager, Ron Saunders, who was born in Birkenhead. —David Coleman, commentator

Horse Racing and Other Equestrian Sports

I don't have any immediate thoughts at the moment.

—Walter Swinburn, British jockey, when asked about his immediate thoughts

· · · · ·

[Jockey] Steve Cauthen, well on his way to that mythical 200 mark. —Jimmy Lindley, commentator

· · · · ·

A RACING HORSE IS NOT LIKE A MACHINE. IT HAS TO BE TUNED UP LIKE A RACING CAR.

—Chris Pool, commentator

· · · · ·

These two horses have met five times this season, and I think they've beaten each other on each occasion. —Jimmy Lindley

. . . in 1900 the owner of the Grand National winner was the then Prince of Wales, King Edward VII.

—David Coleman, commentator

· · · · ·

There's Pam watching anxiously. She doesn't look anxious, though. —Stephen Hadley, British show jumper/commentator

· · · · ·

[Jockey] Tony [McCoy] has a quick look between his legs and likes what he sees. —Stewart Machin

He's a very competitive competitor, that's the sort of competitor he is.

—Dorian Williams, horse show commentator

· · · · ·

As you travel the world, do you do a lot of traveling?

—Harvey Smith, asked of show jumper

· · · · ·

My horse was in the lead, coming down the homestretch, but the caddie fell off. —Samuel Goldwyn, movie producer

· · · · ·

The racecourse is as level as a billiard ball.

—John Francombe, former jockey

Golf

There he stands with his legs akimbo. —Peter Alliss, commentator

· · · · ·

And now to hole eight, which is in fact the eighth hole.

—Peter Alliss

· · · · ·

THIS IS THE 12TH—THE GREEN IS LIKE A PLATEAU WITH THE TOP SHAVED OFF.

—Renton Laidlaw, golf writer/commentator

· · · · ·

I owe a lot to my parents, especially my mother and my father.

—Greg Norman

· · · · ·

I'M A GOLFER—NOT AN ATHLETE.

—Lee Westwood

· · · · ·

He used to be fairly indecisive, but now he's not so certain.

—Peter Alliss

Arnie [Palmer], usually a great putter, seems to be having trouble with his long putt. However, he has no trouble dropping his shorts. —uncredited broadcaster

Track and Field

She hasn't run faster than herself before. —said of Zola Budd

· · · · ·

Born in America, John returned to his native Japan.

—Mike Gratton, commentator

· · · · ·

. . . AND FINALLY, SHE TASTES THE SWEET SMELL OF SUCCESS.

—Ian Edwards, commentator

· · · · ·

A very powerful set of lungs, very much hidden by that chest of his. —Alan Pascoe, commentator

· · · · ·

Be a Good Sport
The Top 7 Bad-Sport Quips from the Playing Field and Beyond

Because good sportsmanship is so elusive. . . .

He has a face like a warthog that's been stung by a wasp.

—David Feherty on fellow golfer Colin Montgomerie

Competitive sports are played mainly on a five-and-a-half-inch court, the space between your ears.

—Bobby Jones

If I could hit the ball that way, I'd take off my toeplate and retire from pitching. In fact, if I hit the way you do, I think I'd also retire from baseball. —baseball pitcher Bob Gibson to teammate Curt Flood during batting practice

[He's] so ugly, when he sweats the sweat runs backwards over his head to avoid his face!

—Muhammad Ali on an opponent

He couldn't bowl a hoop downhill.

—sports commentator Fred Trueman on cricketer Ian Botham

You! You're the child who rhapsodizes about the infield-fly rule. I'm sure you'll have a fine career. —Howard Cosell to sportscaster Bob Costas

She's about as cuddly as a dead hedgehog. The Alsatians in her yard would go about in pairs for protection. —jockey John Francombe on racehorse trainer Jenny Pitman

Britain's last gold medal was a bronze in 1952 in Helsinki.
—Nigel Starmer-Smith, commentator

. . . . .

The Americans sowed the seed, and now they have reaped the whirlwind. —Sebastian Coe, runner

. . . . .

Well Phil, tell us about your amazing third leg.
—Ross King, discussing relays with champion runner Phil Redmond

. . . . .

MARY DECKER SLANEY, THE WORLD'S GREATEST FRONT-RUNNER—I SHOULDN'T BE SURPRISED TO SEE HER AT THE FRONT.

—Ron Pickering, commentator

. . . . .

Watch the time. It gives you an indication of how fast they are running. —Ron Pickering

. . . . .

And the mile once again becomes the focal point, where it's always been. —Ron Pickering

. . . . .

The Americans' heads are on their chins a little bit at the moment. —Ron Pickering

· · · · ·

That's inches away from being millimeter-perfect. —Ted Lowe

Other Sports

And he's got the ice pack on his groin there, so it's possibly not the old shoulder injury. —Ray French, rugby sportscaster

· · · · ·

Venezuela! Great, that's the Italian city with the guys in the boats, right?
—Murad Muhammad, on being told about a boxing match in South America

· · · · ·

AND FOR THOSE OF YOU WATCHING ON BLACK-AND-WHITE, THE PINK BALL IS THE ONE BEHIND THE BLUE. —TV BILLIARDS COMMENTATOR

· · · · ·

I don't want to tell you any half-truths unless they're completely accurate. —Dennis Rappaport, boxing manager

· · · · ·

IT'S ABOUT 90 PERCENT STRENGTH
AND 40 PERCENT TECHNIQUE.

—Johnny Walker, world middleweight wrist-wrestling champion

· · · · ·

There isn't a record in existence that hasn't been broken.

—Chay Blyth, yachtsman

· · · · ·

It's obvious these Russian swimmers are determined to do well on American soil. —Anita Lonsborough, commentator

· · · · ·

Cycling's a good thing for the youngsters, because it keeps them off the streets. —David Bean, commentator

· · · · ·

IN THE REAR, THE SMALL, DIMINUTIVE FIGURE
OF SHOAIF MOHAMMED, WHO CAN'T BE MUCH
TALLER OR SHORTER THAN HE IS.

—Henry Blofeld, cricket commentator

· · · · ·

It's a catch he would have caught 99 times out of 1,000.

—Henry Blofeld

· · · · ·

His throw went absolutely nowhere near where it was going.

—Richie Benaud, cricket commentator

· · · · ·

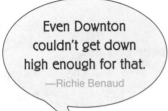

Even Downton couldn't get down high enough for that.

—Richie Benaud

That black cloud is coming from the direction the wind is blowing; now the wind is coming from where the black cloud is. —Ray Illingworth, former cricket player

· · · · ·

I was in a no-win situation, so I'm glad that I won rather than lost. —Frank Bruno, boxer

· · · · ·

THE LEAD CAR IS ABSOLUTELY UNIQUE, EXCEPT FOR THE ONE BEHIND IT WHICH IS IDENTICAL.

—Murray Walker

· · · · ·

THERE HAVE BEEN INJURIES AND DEATHS IN BOXING, BUT NONE OF THEM SERIOUS.

—Alan Minter, former prizefighter

· · · · ·

We now have exactly the same situation as we had at the start of the race, only exactly the opposite.

—Murray Walker, auto race announcer

· · · · ·

The Queen's Park Oval, exactly as its name suggests, is absolutely round. —Tony Crozier, sportscaster

· · · · ·

That's so when I forget how to spell my name, I can still find my clothes. —Stu Grimson, Chicago Blackhawks hockey player, on why he keeps a color photo of himself above his locker

· · · · ·

WE HAVE ONLY ONE PERSON TO BLAME, AND THAT'S EACH OTHER.

—Barry Beck, New York Ranger, explaining a championship game brawl

· · · · ·

If I wasn't talking, I wouldn't know what to say.

—Chico Resch, New York Islanders goalie

· · · · ·

I'M GLAD YOU'RE DOING THIS STORY ON US AND NOT ON THE WNBA. WE'RE SO MUCH PRETTIER THAN ALL THE OTHER WOMEN IN SPORTS.

—Martina Hingis, tennis player

· · · · ·

It's a nice bonus but, you know, I have to pay taxes too.

—Venus Williams, tennis player, after winning the Grand Slam Cup

· · · · ·

He's a guy who gets up at six o'clock in the morning regardless of what time it is. —Lou Duva, boxing trainer

· · · · ·

It's basically the same, just darker. —Alan Kulwicki, stock car racer, on racing at night instead of during the afternoon

· · · · ·

ON WHAT?

—boxer Chris Eubank, when asked whether he thought about writing his autobiography

· · · · ·

We've got to pause and ask ourselves: How much clean air do we need?

—Lee Iacocca, former chairman,
Ford Motor Company

Chapter 16

Global Industry

I n the medium of global industry, there are no boundaries. Enjoy the following imperfect views of the world yesterday, today, and tomorrow.

Astronomy

Jupiter's moons are invisible to the naked eye, and therefore can have no influence on the earth, and therefore would be useless, and therefore do not exist.

—contemporaries of Galileo Galilei, circa 1610

. . . . . .

The proposition, that the sun is the centre and does not revolve about the earth, is foolish, absurd, false in theology and heretical. —The Inquisition, on Galileo's theories

. . . . . .

Comets are not heavenly bodies, but originate in the earth's atmosphere below the moon. —Father Augustin de Angelis, 1673

. . . . . .

Medicine

I heard Harvey say that after his book came out, he fell mightily in his practice. 'Twas believed by the vulgar that he was crackbrained, and all the physicians were against him. I knew several doctors in London that would not have given threepence for one of his medicines. —John Aubrey, on the reaction to William Harvey's discovery of blood circulation, circa 1630

· · · · ·

... for a man to infect a family in the morning with smallpox and to pray to God in the evening against the disease is blasphemy; that the smallpox is "a judgment of God on the sins of the people," and that "to avert it is but to provoke him more"; that inoculation is "an encroachment on the prerogatives of Jehovah, whose right it is to wound and smite."

—contemporary reaction to inoculation experiments by American physician Dr. Zabdiel Boylston, circa 1720

· · · · ·

Smallpox is a visitation from God; but the cowpox is produced by presumptuous man; the former was what Heaven ordained, the latter is, perhaps, a daring violation of our holy religion.

—A physician's reaction to Dr. Edward Jenner's experiments in developing a vaccine for smallpox, 1796

· · · · ·

LOUIS PASTEUR'S THEORY OF GERMS IS RIDICULOUS FICTION.

—Pierre Pachet, professor of physiology, University of Toulouse, 1872

The abolishment of pain in surgery is a chimera. It is absurd to go on seeking it today. "Knife" and "pain" are two words in surgery that must forever be associated in the consciousness of the patient. To this compulsory combination we shall have to adjust ourselves. —Alfred Velpeau, decrying the use of anesthesia, 1839

. . . . .

... must be portions of the human frame that will ever remain sacred from its intrusions, at least in the surgeon's hands. That we have already, if not quite, reached these final limits, there can be little question. The abdomen, the chest, and the brain will be forever shut from the intrusion of the wise and humane surgeon.

—Sir John Eric Ericksen, Surgeon-Extraordinaire to Queen Victoria, 1873

Electricity

... he who looks on the world with the eye of reverence must turn aside from this book as the result of an incurable delusion, whose sole effort is to detract from the dignity of nature.

—a critic's reaction to George Simon Ohm's theory of electricity, 1827

... a physicist who professed such heresies was unworthy to teach science.

—unrecorded German minister of education, referring to Ohm

. . . . .

Just as certain as death, [George] Westinghouse will kill a customer within six months after he puts in a system of any size. —Thomas A. Edison

. . . . .

Thomas Edison's ideas of developing an incandescent lamp may be good enough for our transatlantic friends . . . but unworthy of the attention of practical or scientific men. . . . I do not think there is the slightest chance of its [electricity] competing, in a general way, with gas. There are defects about the electric light which, unless some essential change takes place, must entirely prevent its application to ordinary lighting purposes.

—Select Committee on Lighting by Electricity, British House of Commons, 1879

Communications

I watched his countenance closely, to see if he was not deranged . . . and I was assured by other senators after we left the room that they had no confidence in it. —Senator Smith of Indiana after Samuel Morse demonstrated his telegraph, 1842

· · · · ·

. . . What was this telegraph to do? Would it transmit letters and newspapers? And besides, the telegraph might be made very mischievous, and secret information thereafter communicated to the prejudice of merchants.

—Senator George McDuffie, on an amendment to allocate funds to construct a telegraph line between Baltimore and New York City, 1845

· · · · ·

The operation of the telegraph between Washington and Baltimore had not satisfied [me] that under any rate of postage that could be adopted, its revenues could be made equal to its expenditures. —Postmaster General Cave Johnson, when Samuel Morse tried to sell the rights to the telegraph to the U.S. Post Office (date unknown)

... As far as I can judge, I do not look upon any system of wireless telegraphy as a serious competitor with our cables. Some years ago I said the same thing and nothing has since occurred to alter my views. —Sir John Wolfe-Barry to stockholders of the Western Telegraph Company, 1907

· · · · ·

THE WIRELESS MUSIC BOX HAS NO IMAGINABLE COMMERCIAL VALUE. WHO WOULD PAY FOR A MESSAGE SENT TO NOBODY IN PARTICULAR?

—associates of RCA chairman David Sarnoff, in response
to his suggestion that the corporation invest in
radio technology, circa 1920

· · · · ·

... You could put in this room, de Forest, all the radiotelephone apparatus that the country will ever need!

—W. W. Dean, president of the Dean Telephone Company, to Lee de Forest,
inventor of the vacuum tube and "father" of television, 1907

· · · · ·

De Forest has said in many newspapers and over his signature that it would be possible to transmit human voice across the Atlantic before many years. Based on these absurd and deliberately misleading statements, the misguided public ... has been persuaded to purchase stock in his company. ...

—Prosecutor in the 1913 stock fraud trial of Lee de Forest [De Forest was acquitted, but the judge advised him to get a "common garden variety of job and stick to it"]

· · · · ·

Through the Ages

The story of the birth of civilization is, at times, fascinating and, at times, droll. History's many defining moments—steps forward and backward—are good and bad. There are things to commemorate and things to forget. But the timelessness of a witty Q&A is to be enjoyed over and over again.

Q: What do you call a handcuffed man?

A: Trustworthy.

Q: Why do only 10 percent of men make it to heaven?

A: Because if they all went, it would be Hell.

Q: Why do men like smart women?

A: Opposites attract.

Q: How many men does it take to screw in a lightbulb?

A: One. He just holds it up there and waits for the world to revolve around him.

Q: Why is psychoanalysis a lot quicker for men than for women?

A: When it's time to go back to his childhood, he's already there.

Q: What do you do with a bachelor who thinks he's God's gift to women?

A: Exchange him.

Q: What should you give a man who has everything?

A: A woman to show him how to work it.

Q: What's a man's idea of honesty in a relationship?

A: Telling you his real name.

Q: What's the best way to force a man to do sit ups?

A: Put the remote control between his toes.

Q: Why did God create man before woman?

A: Because you're always supposed to have a rough draft before creating your masterpiece.

Well, then of what possible use can your "radiotelephone" be? It can't compare with the wire phone, you say, and it can't cover the distances that the wireless telegraph can cover. Then what the hell use is it anyway, Lee?

—unidentified friend of de Forest

Theory of Evolution

My recent studies have made me more adverse than ever to the new scientific doctrines [Charles Darwin's theory of evolution] which are flourishing now in England. This sensational zeal reminds me of what I experienced as a young man in Germany, when the physiophilosophy of Oken had invaded every centre of scientific activity; and yet, what is there left of it? I trust to outlive this mania also.

—Louis Agassiz, circa 1870

· · · · ·

ALL THAT WAS NEW IN THEM WAS FALSE, AND ALL THAT WAS TRUE IN THEM WAS OLD.

—Professor Haughton of the University of Dublin, commenting on Darwin's findings, circa 1870

· ·

327

Transportation

It is far from my wish to promulgate to the world that
the ridiculous expectations, or rather professions, of the
enthusiastic speculist will be realised, and that we shall
see them travelling at the rate of 12, 16, 18, or 20 miles an
hour: nothing could do more harm towards their adoption,
or general improvement, than the promulgation of such
nonsense. —Nicolas Wood, 1825

· · · · ·

. . . that any general systems of conveying passengers would
answer, to go at a velocity exceeding 10 miles an hour, or
thereabouts, is extremely improbable. —Thomas Tredgold, 1835

· · · · ·

It was declared that its formation would prevent cows grazing
and hens laying. The poisoned air from the locomotives would
kill birds as they flew over them, and render the preservation
of pheasants and foxes no longer possible. Householders
adjoining the projected line were told that their houses would
be burnt up by the fire thrown from the engine-chimneys,
while the air around would be polluted by clouds of smoke.
There would no longer be any use for horses; and if railways
extended, the species would become extinguished, and oats
and hay unsalable commodities. Traveling by road would
be rendered highly dangerous, and country inns would be
ruined. Boilers would burst and blow passengers to atoms. But
there was always this consolation to wind up with—that the
weight of the locomotive would completely prevent its moving,
and that railways, even if made, could never be worked by
steam-power! —pamphlets opposing the use of railroads in Britain, 1823

... a pretty plan; but there is just one point overlooked—that the steam engine requires a firm basis on which to work!

—Sir Joseph Banks, explorer-naturalist and president of the Royal Society, on applying steam engines on ships, circa 1800

· · · · ·

... even if the propeller had the power of propelling a vessel, it would be found altogether useless in practice, because the power being applied in the stern it would be absolutely impossible to make the vessel steer. —Sir William Symonds, Surveyor of the British Navy, on the idea of powering a ship by means of a screw propeller, 1837

· · · · ·

The actual building of roads devoted to motor cars is not for the near future, in spite of many rumors to that effect.

—article in *Harper's Weekly*, 1902

· · · · ·

Airplanes are interesting toys but of no military value. —Ferdinand Foch, professor of strategy, French Army College, circa 1905 [Foch later became Allied Supreme Commander during World War I]

Heavier-than-air flying machines are impossible.
—Lord Kelvin, president of the Royal Society, 1895

· · · · ·

The Edison Company offered me the general superintendency of the company but only on condition that I would give up my gas engine and devote myself to something really useful.

—Henry Ford (in his memoirs)

Warfare

The bow is a simple weapon; firearms are very complicated things which get out of order in many ways. . . . . a very heavy weapon and tires out soldiers on the march. Whereas also a bowman can let off six aimed shots a minute, a musketeer can discharge but one in two minutes. —Colonel Sir John Smyth opposing the change from the longbow to musketry, 1591

· · · · ·

"What shall I do with the machine-guns today, sir?" would be the question frequently asked by the officer in charge of a field day. "Take the damn things to a flank and hide them!" was the usual reply. —Brigadier-General Baker-Carr, British Army, on the dislike of machine guns by battalion commanders, 1914

· · · · ·

That Professor Goddard with his "chair" in Clark College and the countenancing of the Smithsonian Institution does not know the relation of action to reaction, and of the need to have something better than a vacuum against which to react—to say that would be absurd. Of course he only seems to lack the knowledge ladled out daily in high schools . . .

—editorial in the New York Times on Robert Goddard, "father" of American rocket science, 1921

· · · · ·

I WOULD MUCH PREFER TO HAVE GODDARD INTERESTED IN REAL SCIENTIFIC DEVELOPMENT THAN TO HAVE HIM PRIMARILY INTERESTED IN MORE SPECTACULAR ACHIEVEMENTS WHICH ARE OF LESS REAL VALUE

—Charles A. Lindbergh, 1936

· · · · ·

The day of the battleship has not passed, and it is highly unlikely that an airplane, or fleet of them, could ever successfully sink a fleet of Navy vessels under battle conditions. —Franklin D. Roosevelt, Assistant Secretary of the Navy, 1922

· · · · ·

The editor of *Scientific American* wrote that this idea [a rocket-accelerated airplane bomb] was . . . too far-fetched to be considered.

—Willy Ley, astronautics expert, 1940

. . . As far as sinking a ship with a bomb is concerned, you just can't do it.

—U.S. Rear Admiral Clark Woodward, 1939

· · · · ·

People have been talking about a 3,000-mile high-angle rocket shot from one continent to another, carrying an atomic bomb and so directed as to be a precise weapon. . . . I say, technically, I don't think anyone in the world knows how to do such a thing, and I feel confident that it will not be done for a very long period of time to come.

—Dr. Vannevar Bush on developing intercontinental missiles, 1945

· · · · ·

Man will never reach the moon regardless of all future scientific advances. —Lee de Forest, circa 1950

Canals

All mankind has heard much of M. de Lesseps and his Suez Canal . . . I have a very strong opinion that such canal will not and cannot be made; that all the strength of the arguments adduced in the matter are hostile to it; and that steam navigation by land will and ought to be the means of transit through Egypt.

—Anthony Trollope on Ferdinand de Lesseps, designer of the Suez Canal, 1860

· · · · ·

THE PANAMA CANAL IS ACTUALLY A THING OF THE PAST, AND NATURE IN HER WORKS WILL SOON OBLITERATE ALL TRACES OF FRENCH ENERGY AND MONEY EXPENDED ON THE ISTHMUS.

—article in *Scientific American*, 1941

Atomic Energy

I can accept the theory of relativity as little as I can accept the existence of atoms and other such dogma. —Ernst Mach, circa 1930

· · · · ·

The energy produced by the breaking down of the atom is a very poor kind of thing. Anyone who looks for a source of power in the transformation of the atom is talking moonshine.
—Sir Ernest Rutherford, 1933

· · · · ·

ATOMIC ENERGY MIGHT BE AS GOOD AS OUR PRESENT-DAY EXPLOSIVES, BUT IT IS UNLIKELY TO PRODUCE ANYTHING VERY MUCH MORE DANGEROUS.
—Sir Winston Churchill, 1939

· · · · ·

That is the biggest fool thing we have ever done. . . . The bomb will never go off, and I speak as an expert in explosives.
—Admiral William Leahy to President Harry S Truman
regarding the atomic bomb, 1945

· · · · ·

Computers

I think there is a world market for maybe five computers.
—Thomas Watson, chairman of the board, IBM, 1943

· · · · ·

COMPUTERS IN THE FUTURE MAY WEIGH NO MORE THAN 1.5 TONS.
—*Popular Mechanics*, 1949

· · · · ·

I have traveled the length and breadth of this country and talked with the best people, and I can assure you that data processing is a fad that won't last out the year.
—editor of business books, Prentice Hall publishers, 1957

· · · · ·

But what . . . is it [a microchip] good for?
—engineer at the Advanced Computing Systems Division of IBM, 1968

· · · · ·

THERE IS NO REASON ANYONE WOULD WANT A COMPUTER IN THEIR HOME.
—Ken Olson, founder of Digital Equipment Corp., 1972

· · · · ·

Border Battles
The Best of the Best International Insults

Can't we all just get along? In the interest of global unity, can we unite with our fellow man or will we continue to make goofy gaffes? In the end, it really doesn't matter what country you reside in, so take the time to enjoy these silly snippets.

I found the pearl of the Orient slightly less exciting than a rainy Sunday evening in Rochester.
—S. J. Perelman

Unmitigated noodles.
—Kaiser Wilhelm II on England

Canada could have had French culture, American know-how, and English government. Instead it got French government, English know-how, and American culture. —John Colombo

Paris is like a whore, from a distance she seems ravishing, you can't wait until you have her in your arms. Five minutes later you feel empty, disgusted with yourself. You feel tricked.
—Henry Miller

If one could teach the English to talk and the Irish to listen, society would be quite civilized.
—Oscar Wilde

The Japanese have perfected good manners and made them indistinguishable from rudeness.
—Paul Theroux

In America, only the successful writer is important, in France all writers are important, in England no writer is important, and in Australia you have to explain what a writer is.
—Geoffrey Cottrell

Germans are flummoxed by humor, the Swiss have no concept of fun, the Spanish think there is nothing at all ridiculous about eating dinner at midnight, and the Italians should never, ever have been let in on the invention of the motor car. —Bill Bryson

Rome reminds me of a man who lives by exhibiting to travelers his grandmother's corpse.
—James Joyce

We went to Atari and said, "Hey, we've got this amazing thing, even built with some of your parts, and what do you think about funding us?" They said, "No." So then we went to Hewlett-Packard, and they said, "We don't need you. You haven't got through college yet." —Apple Computer, Inc. founder Steve Jobs, on attempts to interest the two corporations in a personal computer that he and Steve Wozniak had developed

∎ ∎ ∎ ∎ ∎

"640K" OUGHT TO BE ENOUGH [COMPUTER MEMORY] FOR ANYBODY.

—Bill Gates, Microsoft founder, 1981

∎ ∎ ∎ ∎ ∎

One hundred million dollars is way too much to pay for Microsoft. —unidentified IBM executive, 1982

Other Inventions and Business

The trade of Advertising is now so near to perfection that it is not easy to propose any improvement. —The Idler, 1759

∎ ∎ ∎ ∎ ∎

[They] might as well try to light London with a slice from the moon. —William H. Wollaston, English chemist, commenting on a proposal to light British cities with gas lamps, circa 1800

∎ ∎ ∎ ∎ ∎

DRILL FOR OIL? YOU MEAN DRILL INTO THE GROUND TO TRY AND FIND OIL? YOU'RE CRAZY.

—workers whom Edwin L. Drake tried to hire on his project to drill for oil in Titusville, Pennsylvania, 1859

* * * * *

Stocks have reached what looks like a permanently high plateau. —Irving Fisher, professor of economics, Yale University, 1929

* * * * *

The concept is interesting and well formed, but in order to earn better than a "C," the idea must be feasible. —a professor of management at Yale University, commenting on the term paper by Fred Smith (which earned a "C") that outlined a plan for a reliable overnight delivery service; Smith went on to found Federal Express in 1973

* * * * *

A cookie store is a bad idea. Besides, the market research reports say America likes crispy cookies, not soft and chewy cookies like you make.

—unidentified response to Debbi Fields's plan to start Mrs. Fields Cookies

* * * * *

If I had thought about it, I wouldn't have done the experiment. The literature was full of examples that said you can't do this.

—Spencer Silver on the work that led to the adhesives for 3M Post-it notepads

·····

You want to have consistent and uniform muscle development across all of your muscles? It can't be done. It's just a fact of life. You just have to accept inconsistent muscle development as an unalterable condition of weight training.

—response to Arthur Jones, who went on to invent Nautilus fitness machines.

·····

Everything that can be invented has been invented.

—Charles H. Duell, commissioner, U.S. Office of Patents, 1899

... The advancement of the arts from year to year taxes our credulity and seems to presage the arrival of that period when further improvements must end.

—Henry L. Ellsworth, commissioner, U.S. Office of Patents, 1844

·····

I TELL YOU, IT'S BIG BUSINESS. IF THERE'S ONE WORD TO DESCRIBE ATLANTIC CITY, IT'S BIG BUSINESS. OR TWO WORDS—BIG BUSINESS.

—Donald Trump, as quoted in a 1989 *Time* magazine article

·····

This company is not bust. We are merely in a cyclical decline.

—Lord Stokes, chairman of British Leyland, 1974

• • • • •

You can't just let nature run wild!

—Walter Hickel, governor of Alaska, on a plan to kill wolves

• • • • •

IF YOU SET ASIDE THREE MILE ISLAND AND CHERNOBYL, THE SAFETY RECORD OF NUCLEAR ENERGY IS REALLY VERY GOOD.

—Paul O'Neill, secretary of the Treasury

• • • • •

That's Paris, Ontario,
not Paris, Italy.

—host of a Canadian children's
television show

Chapter 17
Media Medley

I f it's in the news, it has to be true, right? Decide for yourself with this plethora of quotes garnered from the media for your reading enjoyment.

At the present moment, the whole fleet is lit up. When I say "lit up," I mean lit up by fairy lamps. It's fantastic. It isn't a fleet at all. It's just . . . It's fairyland. The whole fleet is in fairyland. Now, if you'll follow me through . . . the next few moments you'll find the fleet doing odd things. —Lieutenant Commander Tommy Woodroofe describing the "illumination" of the Royal Navy fleet at Spithead, 1937 (it seems the commentator was also well lit up)

· · · · · ·

I THINK I KNOW THAT ONE. IS IT JEWISH?

—quiz show contestant when asked for the Pope's religion

· · · · · ·

Shergar. —contestant on the television quiz show, *The Weakest Link*, when asked which famous racehorse's name was the word "murder" spelled backward

· · · · · ·

A memorial has been set up for the victims of the atrocity outside the west door of Westminster Abbey. —BBC broadcast

· · · · ·

The telephone company is urging people not to use the telephone unless it is absolutely necessary, in order to keep the lines open for emergency calls. We'll be right back after this break to give away a pair of Phil Collins concert tickets to caller number 95.

—unidentified radio disc jockey after the 1990 Los Angeles earthquake

· · · · ·

Who the hell wants to hear actors talk? —Harry Warner of Warner Brothers movie studio, when asked about sound in films

· · · · ·

ROTARIANS, BE PATRIOTIC! LEARN TO SHOOT YOURSELF.

—Chicago Rotary Club journal, Gyrator

· · · · ·

The crime bill passed by the senate would reinstate the federal death penalty for certain violent crimes: assassinating the President; hijacking an airliner; and murdering a government poultry inspector. —Knight Ridder News Service dispatch

· · · · ·

The farmers in Annapolis Valley are pleased to announce that this year there will be an abundance of apples. This is particularly good news because most of the farmers haven't had a good crap in years.

—unidentified Maryland television news broadcaster

· · · · ·

Ladies and gentlemen . . . and now Mr. Eddie Playbody will pee for you. —radio announcer introducing banjoist, Eddie Peabody

· · · · ·

Sir Stifford Craps. —Lowell Thomas, radio commentator, presenting the British prime minister, Sir Stafford Cripps

· · · · ·

The Duck and Doochess of Windsor. —unidentified radio announcer referring to the Duke and Duchess of Windsor

· · · · ·

. . . AND FROM WASHINGTON COMES WORD THAT PRESIDENT AND MRS. LINCOLN WILL SPEND NIXON'S BIRTHDAY AT KEY BISCAYNE, FLORIDA, ON FEBRUARY TWELFTH.

—unidentified radio newscaster

· · · · ·

Retraction: The "Greek Special" is a huge, 18-inch pizza and not a huge, 18-inch penis, as described in an ad. Blondie's Pizza would like to apologize for any confusion Friday's ad may have caused. —correction in *The Daily Californian*

· · · · ·

As a prize—a beautiful riding mower with optional ass scratcher! —announcer on television show, who meant to say "grass catcher"

· · · · ·

Then you add two forkfuls of cooking oil . . . —recipe given on television's *The French Chef*

Be with us again next Saturday at 10 P.M. for "High Fidelity," designed to help music lovers increase their reproduction.

—unidentified radio announcer

· · · · ·

When you are thirsty, try 7 UP the refreshing drink in the green bottle with the big 7 on it and u-p after.

—unidentified radio announcer

· · · · ·

ASK US ABOUT OUR CUP SIZE OR OUR FAVORITE POSITION, BUT–PLEASE– NO PERSONAL QUESTIONS.

—twin models, when asked who was older

· · · · ·

To say this book is about me (which is the main reason I was uncomfortable—me, me, me, me, me . . . frightening!) is ridiculous. This book is not about me.

—Kate Moss, model/actress, on her book, *Kate: The Kate Moss Book*

· · · · ·

SMOKING KILLS. IF YOU'RE KILLED, YOU'VE LOST A VERY IMPORTANT PART OF YOUR LIFE.

—Brooke Shields, actress/model, during an interview to front an anti-smoking campaign

· · · · ·

I believe that mink are raised for being turned into fur coats and if we didn't wear fur coats, those little animals would never have been born. So is it better not to have been born, or to have lived for one or two years to have been turned into a fur coat? I don't know. —Barbi Benton, model and actress

· · · · ·

It's not listed in the Bible, but my spiritual gift, my specific calling from God, is to be a television talk show host.

—James Bakker, televangelist

· · · · ·

Please accept my resignation. I don't care to belong to any club that will have me as a member.

—Groucho Marx, in a letter written to the owner of a Hollywood club

· · · · ·

Whenever I watch TV and see those poor starving kids all over the world, I can't help but cry. I mean, I'd love to be skinny like that, but not with all those flies and death and stuff. —Mariah Carey, singer

* * * * *

I DON'T FEEL WE DID WRONG IN TAKING THIS GREAT COUNTRY AWAY FROM THEM. THERE WERE GREAT NUMBERS OF PEOPLE WHO NEEDED NEW LAND, AND THE INDIANS WERE SELFISHLY TRYING TO KEEP IT FOR THEMSELVES.

—John Wayne

* * * * *

TV won't be able to hold any market after the first six months. People will soon get tired of staring at a plywood box every night. —Darryl Zanuck, head of 20th Century Fox movie studios, 1946

* * * * *

Movies are a fad. Audiences really want to see live actors on a stage. —Charlie Chaplin

* * * * *

I'm just glad it'll be Clark Gable who's falling on his face, and not Gary Cooper. —Gary Cooper, on his decision not to take the leading role in *Gone With the Wind*

* * * * *

"You can quote me!"

Special care should be taken with the news to leave the reader with a unique feel-good note. Well, the following quips are sure to do just that for much can be said about making news, especially when the news says things like these!

An end is in sight to the severe weather shortage.
—TV weatherman

Ladies and gentlemen, now you can have a bikini for a ridiculous figure.
—Radio announcer

Well, here it is Christmas. So we have a skeleton screw, er, skeleton crew here today.
—Radio announcer

Red squirrels . . . you don't see many of them since they became extinct.
—British Radio 2 announcer

If it weren't for electricity, we'd all be watching television by candlelight.
—TV personality

The U.S. may increase aid to the former Soviet Union by as much as a billion dollars to help stabilize the rubble.
—Radio news report confusing ruble with "rubble"

We now will hear "Deck Your Balls with Halls of Helly" . . . "Deck your Bell with Balls of Holly" . . . er . . . a Christmas selection.
—BBC radio announcer

• •

347

As a mother, I know that homosexuals cannot biologically reproduce children; therefore, they must recruit our children.

—Anita Bryant

. . . . .

The government is not doing enough about cleaning up the environment. This is a good planet. —Mr. New Jersey contestant, when asked what he would do with a million dollars

. . . . .

ROCK 'N' ROLL IS PHONY AND FALSE, AND SUNG, WRITTEN, AND PLAYED FOR THE MOST PART BY CRETINOUS GOONS.

—Frank Sinatra, 1957

. . . . .

We don't like their sound, and guitar music is on the way out.

—Decca Recording Company executive, turning down the Beatles, 1962

Real Newspaper Headlines

Police Suspicious After Body
Found in Graveyard

• • • • •

Male Infertility Can Be Passed
on to Children

• • • • •

Statistics Show that Mortality
Increases Perceptibly in the
Military During Wartime

• • • • •

INCLUDE YOUR CHILDREN
WHEN BAKING COOKIES

• • • • •

Something Went Wrong in Jet Crash,
Experts Say

• • • • •

Police Begin Campaign to
Run Down Jaywalkers

• • • • •

Drunks Get Nine Months
in Violin Case

· · · · ·

Iraqi Head Seeks Arms

· · · · ·

Prostitutes Appeal to Pope

· · · · ·

Panda Mating Fails;
Veterinarian Takes Over

· · · · ·

British Left Waffles on
Falkland Islands

· · · · ·

Clinton Wins Budget; More Lies Ahead

· · · · ·

PLANE TOO CLOSE TO GROUND, CRASH PROBE TOLD

· · · · ·

Real Newspaper
Headlines

Miners Refuse to Work After Death

. . . . . .

Juvenile Court to Try Shooting Defendant

. . . . . .

STOLEN PAINTING FOUND BY TREE

. . . . . .

Two Sisters Reunited After
18 Years in Checkout Counter

. . . . . .

War Dims Hope for Peace

. . . . . .

COUPLE SLAIN; POLICE SUSPECT HOMICIDE

. . . . . .

Man Struck by Lightning
Faces Battery Charge

. . . . . .

Astronaut Takes Blame for Gas in Space

. . . . . .

New Study of Obesity Looks
for Larger Test Group

· · · · ·

Kids Make Nutritious Snacks

· · · · ·

LOCAL HIGH SCHOOL DROPOUTS
CUT IN HALF

· · · · ·

Typhoon Rips through Cemetery;
Hundreds Dead

· · · · ·

Deaf Mute Gets New Hearing
in Killing

· · · · ·

House Passes Gas Tax on to Senate

· · · · ·

STIFF OPPOSITION EXPECTED TO
CASKETLESS FUNERAL PLAN

· · · · ·

Real Newspaper
Headlines

TWO CONVICTS EVADE NOOSE, JURY HUNG

· · · · ·

William Kelly Was Fed Secretary

· · · · ·

Milk Drinkers Are Turning to Powder

· · · · ·

SAFETY EXPERTS SAY SCHOOL BUS PASSENGERS SHOULD BE BELTED

· · · · ·

Farmer Bill Dies in House

· · · · ·

Queen Mary Having Bottom Scraped

· · · · ·

NJ Judge to Rule on Nude Beach

· · · · ·

Child's Stool Great for Use in Garden

· · · · ·

Media Slurs

Slurs left and right quiet opponents. Or do they? Doesn't it set off media frenzy instead? Vultures swarming over the not-so-dead carcass of the badly battered. But isn't character assassination fun? Admit it; you enjoy a good verbal sparring now and again. So enjoy the turnabout as members of the press receive their comeuppance.

A journalist is a person who works harder than any other lazy person in the world. —Anonymous

The only qualities for real success in journalism are ratlike cunning, a plausible manner and a little literary ability.

—Nicholas Tomalin

If a person is not talented enough to be a novelist, not smart enough to be a lawyer, and his hands are too shaky to perform operations, he becomes a journalist.

—Norman Mailer

Your connection with any newspaper would be a disgrace and degradation. I would rather sell gin to poor people and poison them that way.

—Sir Walter Scott to a journalist friend

Archibald Forbes rarely waited for the end of a battle to report it and sometimes did not even wait for the beginning.

—R. J. Cruickshank, editor of the *Daily News* describing Forbes, the paper's famous war correspondent of the 1870s and 1880s.

The fact that a man is a newspaper reporter is evidence of some flaw of character.

—Lyndon Baines Johnson

The lowest depth to which people can sink before God is defined by the word "journalist." If I were a father and had a daughter who was seduced I should despair over her; I would hope for her salvation. But if I had a son who became a journalist and continued to be one for five years, I would give him up.

—Søren Kierkegaard

Quarter of a Million Chinese
Live on Water

. . . . .

Dr. Ruth to Talk about Sex with
Newspaper Editors

. . . . .

Soviet Virgin Lands Short of Goal Again

. . . . .

EYE DROPS OFF SHELF

. . . . .

Squad Helps Dog Bite Victim

. . . . .

Dealers Will Hear Car Talk at Noon

. . . . .

ENRAGED COW INJURES FARMER WITH AX

. . . . .

Lawmen from Mexico Barbecue Guests

. . . . .

Real Newspaper
Headlines

Illiterate? Write Today for Free Help

· · · · ·

Never Withhold Herpes from Loved One

· · · · ·

DRUNK DRIVERS PAID $1,000 IN 1984

· · · · ·

Autos Killing 110 a Day;
Let's Resolve to Do Better

· · · · ·

If Strike Isn't Settled Quickly
It May Last a While

· · · · ·

COLD WAVE LINKED TO TEMPERATURES

· · · · ·

Real Newspaper
Headlines

Child's Death Ruins Couple's Holiday

* * * * *

"Light" Meals Are Lower in Fat, Calories

* * * * *

Smokers Are Productive,
But Death Cuts Efficiency

* * * * *

Blind Woman Gets New Kidney from
Dad She Hasn't Seen in Years

* * * * *

Death Causes Loneliness,
Feeling of Isolation

* * * * *

Whatever Their Motives, Moms Who Kill
Kids Still Shock Us

* * * * *

SURVEY FINDS DIRTIER SUBWAYS
AFTER CLEANING JOBS WERE CUT

* * * * *

Larger Kangaroos Leap Farther,
Researchers Find

· · · · ·

ALCOHOL ADS PROMOTE DRINKING

· · · · ·

Malls Try to Attract Shoppers

· · · · ·

Man Shoots Neighbor With Machete

· · · · ·

LOW WAGES SAID KEY TO POVERTY

· · · · ·

Dirty-Air Cities Far Deadlier
than Clean Ones, Study Shows

· · · · ·

Discoveries: Older Blacks
Have Edge in Longevity

· · · · ·

Man Run Over by Freight Train Dies

Real Newspaper
Headlines

Scientists See Quakes in LA Future

TOMATOES COME IN BIG, LITTLE, MEDIUM SIZES

Wachtler Tells Graduates that Life
in Jail Is Demeaning

Prosecution Paints O.J. as a Wife-Killer

Bible Church's Focus Is the Bible

ECONOMIST USES THEORY
TO EXPLAIN ECONOMY

Clinton Pledges Restraint in
Use of Nuclear Weapons

Court Rules Boxer Shorts
Are Indeed Underwear

Biting Nails Can Be Sign of
Tenseness in a Person

· · · · ·

How We Feel About Ourselves
Is the Core of Self-Esteem

· · · · ·

FISH LURK IN STREAMS

· · · · ·

Lawyer Says Client Is Not That Guilty

· · · · ·

Alzheimer's Center Prepares
for an Affair to Remember

Real Newspaper Classified Ads

One man, seven woman hot tub—$850/
Offer.

· · · · ·

Free: farm kittens. Ready to eat.

· · · · ·

SNOW BLOWER FOR SALE . . .
ONLY USED ON SNOWY DAYS.

· · · · ·

Amana washer $100. Owned by clean bachelor who seldom washed.

· · · · ·

FREE PUPPIES . . .
PART GERMAN SHEPHERD/PART DOG.

· · · · ·

Two wire-mesh butchering gloves, one 5-finger, one 3-finger; pair: $15.

· · · · ·

Cows, calves never bred . . . also 1 gay bull for sale.

· · · · ·

Free puppies: 1/2 cocker spaniel—1/2
sneaky neighbor's dog.

* * * * *

FREE YORKSHIRE TERRIER: 8 YEARS OLD. UNPLEASANT LITTLE DOG.

* * * * *

Full-sized mattress: 20-year warranty.
Like new. Slight urine smell.

* * * * *

Free: 1 can of pork & beans with purchase
of 3 Br 2 Bth Home.

* * * * *

BILL'S SEPTIC CLEANING—"WE HAUL AMERICAN-MADE PRODUCTS."

* * * * *

Found: dirty white dog . . . looks like a rat
. . . been out awhile . . . better be reward.

* * * * *

Real Newspaper
Classified Ads

Get a Little John: The Traveling Urinal—
holds 2 1/2 bottles of beer.

• • • • •

Georgia Peaches—California Grown—89
Cents Lb.

• • • • •

NICE PARACHUTE—NEVER OPENED— USED ONCE—SLIGHTLY STAINED.

• • • • •

American flag—60 stars—pole
included—$100.

• • • • •

Notice: To person or persons who took
the large pumpkin on Highway 87 near
Southridge Storage. Please return the
pumpkin and be checked. Pumpkin may
be radioactive. All other plants in vicinity
are dead.

• • • • •

Our sofa seats the whole mob—and it's made of 100% Italian leather.

·····

JOINING NUDIST COLONY, MUST SELL WASHER & DRYER–$300.

·····

Open House—Body Shapers Toning Salon—Free Coffee & Donuts.

·····

Fully cooked boneless smoked man— $2.09 Lb.

·····

DINNER SPECIAL–TURKEY $2.35; CHICKEN OR BEEF $2.25; CHILDREN $2.00.

·····

Real Newspaper
Classified Ads

For sale: an antique desk suitable for lady with thick legs and large drawers.

·····

For sale: a quilted high chair that can be made into a table, potty-chair, rocking horse, refrigerator, spring coat, size 8 and fur collar.

·····

NOW IS YOUR CHANCE TO HAVE YOUR EARS PIERCED AND GET AN EXTRA PAIR TO TAKE HOME, TOO.

·····

Wanted: 50 girls for stripping machine operators in factory.

·····

No matter what your topcoat is made of, this miracle spray will make it really repellent.

·····

Vacation Special: have your home exterminated.

·····

Seven ounces of choice sirloin steak, boiled to your likeness and smothered with golden fried onion rings.

. . . . .

TIRED OF CLEANING YOURSELF? LET ME DO IT.

. . . . .

Twenty dozen bottles of excellent Old Tawny Port, sold to pay for charges, the owner having lost sight of, and bottled by us last year.

. . . . .

DOG FOR SALE: EATS ANYTHING AND IS FOND OF CHILDREN.

. . . . .

The hotel has bowling alleys, tennis courts, comfortable beds, and other athletic facilities.

. . . . .

Get rid of aunts: Zap does the job in 24 hours.

. . . . .

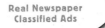

Real Newspaper
Classified Ads

TOASTER: A GIFT THAT EVERY MEMBER OF THE FAMILY APPRECIATES. AUTOMATICALLY BURNS TOAST.

· · · · ·

Sheer stockings: Designed for fancy dress, but so serviceable that lots of women wear nothing else.

· · · · ·

Stock up and save. Limit: one.

· · · · ·

Save regularly in our bank. You'll never regret it. We build bodies that last a lifetime.

· · · · ·

For rent: 6-room hated apartment.

· · · · ·

This is the model home for your future. It was panned by *Better Homes and Gardens*.

. . . . .

MAN, HONEST. WILL TAKE ANYTHING.

. . . . .

Wanted: chambermaid in rectory. Love in, $200 a month. References required.

. . . . .

Wanted: Part-time married girls for soda fountain in sandwich shop.

. . . . .

MAN WANTED TO WORK IN DYNAMITE FACTORY. MUST BE WILLING TO TRAVEL.

. . . . .

Real Newspaper
Classified Ads

Used cars: Why go elsewhere to be cheated? Come here first!

· · · · ·

Christmas tag sale: handmade gifts for the hard-to-find person.

· · · · ·

MODULAR SOFAS: ONLY $299. FOR REST OR FORE PLAY.

· · · · ·

Wanted: Hair-cutter. Excellent growth potential.

· · · · ·

Wanted: Man to take care of cow that does not smoke or drink.

· · · · ·

OUR EXPERIENCED MOM WILL CARE FOR YOUR CHILD. FENCED YARD, MEALS, AND SMACKS INCLUDED.

· · · · ·

AUTO REPAIR SERVICE: FREE PICK-UP AND DELIVERY. TRY US ONCE, YOU'LL NEVER GO ANYWHERE AGAIN.

· · · · ·

See ladies blouses. 50% off! Holcross pullets. Starting to lay Betty Clayton.

· · · · ·

Wanted: Preparer of food. Must be dependable, like the food business, and be willing to get hands dirty.

· · · · ·

WANTED: WIDOWER WITH SCHOOL-AGE CHILDREN REQUIRES PERSON TO ASSUME GENERAL HOUSEKEEPING DUTIES. MUST BE CAPABLE OF CONTRIBUTING TO GROWTH OF FAMILY.

· · · · ·

Mixing bowl set designed to please a cook with round bottom for efficient beating.

· · · · ·

Real Newspaper Classified Ads

Mother's helper—peasant working conditions.

·····

Semi-Annual After-Christmas Sale.

·····

And now, the Superstore—unequaled in size, unmatched in variety, unrivaled inconvenience.

·····

The Second Amendment
gives citizens the right
to bare arms.

Chapter 18

Ludicrous Language

Learning the English language is hard enough without adding in all the jargon. But the following selection of quotes goes beyond normal hum an comprehension.

Malapropisms

Mrs. Malaprop (her name means "inappropriate") was a character in Richard Sheridan's 1775 play, *The Rivals*. She has lent her name to the variety of verbal miscues she came out with, such as:

⋅ ⋅ ⋅ ⋅ ⋅

"Forget this fellow—to *illiterate* him, I say, quite from your memory." [*obliterate*]

⋅ ⋅ ⋅ ⋅ ⋅

"Oh! It gives me the *hydrostatics* to such a degree." [*hysterics*]

⋅ ⋅ ⋅ ⋅ ⋅

"I hope you will represent her to the captain as an object not altogether *illegible*." [*eligible*]

" . . . she might *reprehend* the true meaning of what she is saying." [*comprehend*]

· · · · ·

"I am sorry to say, Sir Anthony, that my *affluence* over my niece is very small." [*influence*]

· · · · ·

"Why, murder's the matter! Slaughter's the matter! Killing's the matter!—But he can tell you the *perpendiculars*." [*particulars*]

· · · · ·

"His *physiognomy* is so grammatical!" [*phraseology*]

· · · · ·

"She's as headstrong as an *allegory* on the banks of the Nile." [*alligator*]

· · · · ·

· ·

374

"I am sure I have done everything in
my power since I *exploded* the affair."
[*exposed*]

· · · · ·

" . . . if ever you betray what you are
entrusted with . . . you forfeit my
malevolence for ever . . ." [*benevolence*]

· · · · ·

"Sure, if I *reprehend* any thing in this
world, it is the use of my *oracular* tongue,
and a nice *derangement* of *epitaphs*!"
[*apprehend, vernacular, arrangement,
epithets*]

Malapropisms from Grade School, High School, and College Examinations

Samuel Morse invented a code for
telepathy.

· · · · ·

The walls of Notre Dame Cathedral are
supported by flying buttocks.

· · · · ·

LOUIS PASTEUR DISCOVERED
A CURE FOR RABBIS.

· · · · ·

In the Renaissance, Martin Luther was nailed to the church door at Wittenberg for selling papal indulgences. He died a horrible death, being excommunicated by a bull.

· · · · ·

The painter Donatello's interest in the female nude made him the father of the Renaissance.

· · · · ·

GUTENBERG INVENTED THE BIBLE.

· · · · ·

Sir Francis Drake circumcised the world with a 100-foot clipper.

· · · · ·

Bach was the most famous composer in the world and so was Handel. Handel was half German, half Italian, and half English.

Malapropisms Found on Student Exams

Johann Sebastian Bach wrote a great many musical compositions and had a large number of children. In between, he practiced on the old spinster which he kept up in his attic.

· · · · ·

Pharaoh forced the Hebrew slaves to make bread without straw.

· · · · ·

Moses led them to the Red Sea, where they made unleavened bread, which is bread made without any ingredients.

· · · · ·

AFTERWARD, MOSES WENT UP ON MOUNT CYANIDE TO GET THE TEN COMMANDMENTS.

· · · · ·

Solomon, one of David's sons, had 500 wives and 500 porcupines.

Wacky Testimony

Jurors are often witness to the stupidity of lawyers. Here are our favorite exchanges from practicing idiots.

Attorney: What is your date of birth?

Witness: July fifteenth.

Attorney: What year?

Witness: Every year.

·

Attorney: This myasthenia gravis—does it affect your memory at all?

Witness: Yes.

Attorney: And in what ways does it affect your memory?

Witness: I forget.

Attorney: You forget. Can you give us an example of something that you've forgotten?

·

Attorney: Now, isn't it true that when a person dies in his sleep, he doesn't know about it until the next morning?

·

Attorney: How far apart were the vehicles at the time of the collision?

·

Witness: Sure, I played for ten years. I even went to school for it.

Attorney: You were there until the time you left, is that true?

·

Attorney: So the date of your baby's conception was August eighth?

Witness: Yes.

Attorney: And what were you doing at that time?

·

Attorney: What did the tissue samples taken from the victim's vagina show?

Witness: There were traces of semen.

Attorney: Male semen?

·

Attorney: You say the stairs went down to the basement?

Witness: Yes.

Attorney: And these stairs, did they go up also?

·

In the Olympic Games, Greeks ran races, jumped, hurled the biscuits, and threw the java. The reward to the victor was a coral wreath.

. . . . .

The government of Athens was democratic because the people took the law into their own hands.

. . . . .

There were no wars in Greece, as the mountains were so high that they couldn't climb over to see what their neighbors were doing.

. . . . .

People have sex, while nouns have genders.

. . . . .

CHRISTMAS IS A TIME FOR HAPPINESS FOR EVERY CHILD, ADULT, AND ADULTERESS.

. . . . .

Women like to do things in circles, where they sew, talk, and do their meddling.

. . . . .

Malapropisms Found on Student Exams

Good punctuation means not to be late.

· · · · ·

THE AMERICAN COLONISTS WON THE REVOLUTIONARY WAR AND NO LONGER HAD TO PAY FOR TAXIS.

· · · · ·

"Don't" is a contraption.

· · · · ·

Italics are what Italians write in.

· · · · ·

Most words are easy to spell once you get the letters write.

· · · · ·

Protons are found in both meat and electricity.

· · · · ·

THE AIR IS THIN HIGH UP IN THE SKY; DOWN HERE, IT'S FAT.

· · · · ·

Malapropisms Found
on Student Exams

Adam and Eve wore nothing but figments.

· · · · ·

Antarctica is like the regular Arctic, but ritzier.

· · · · ·

ABRAHAM LINCOLN BECAME AMERICA'S GREATEST PRECEDENT.

· · · · ·

The bowels are a, e, i, o, u, and sometimes y.

· · · · ·

Guests at Roman banquets wore garlics in their hair.

· · · · ·

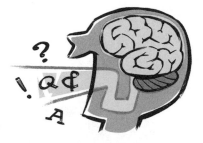

He worked in the government as a civil serpent.

· · · · ·

When a baby is born, the doctor cuts its biblical chord.

· · · · ·

THE FLOOD DAMAGE WAS SO BAD THEY HAD TO EVAPORATE THE CITY.

· · · · ·

Flying saucers are just an optical conclusion.

· · · · ·

Homer wrote *The Oddity*. [*The Odyssey*]

· · · · ·

Malapropisms Found on Student Exams

A horse divided against itself cannot stand.

· · · · ·

THE BRIDE WALKED DOWN THE ISLE.

· · · · ·

Deader than a hangnail.

· · · · ·

Charles Darwin wrote *The Organ of the Species.* [*The Origin of Species*]

· · · · ·

She was as mad as a wet blanket.

· · · · ·

You purify water by filtering it and then forcing it through an aviator.

· · · · ·

EVERYTHING'S FINE—JUST HONKY-TONKY.

· · · · ·

Let dead dogs sleep.

· · · · ·

THE CLIMATE OF THE SARAH DESERT IS SO HOT THAT CERTAIN AREAS ARE CULTIVATED BY IRRITATION.

. . . . .

The U.S. Constitution was adopted to secure domestic hostility.

. . . . .

Columbus discovered America while cursing about the Atlantic.

. . . . .

The doctor felt the man's purse and said there was no hope.

. . . . .

DAMP WEATHER IS VERY HARD ON THE SCIENCES.

. . . . .

The government of England is a limited mockery.

. . . . .

Malapropisms Found on Student Exams

Ignominy

The Top 9 Things A Writer Should Never Hear

Writers have the knack for stringing words together but they become bruised by castigating comments. The following disgraceful quips are words no author should ever hear.

Reading him is like wading through glue.
—Alfred, Lord Tennyson on Ben Jonson

He has never been known to use a word that might send a reader to the dictionary.
—William Faulkner on Ernest Hemingway

I am reading Henry James . . . and feel myself as one entombed in a block of smooth amber.
—Virginia Woolf on Henry James

Poor Faulkner. Does he really think big emotions come from big words?
—Ernest Hemingway on William Faulkner

I have just read a long novel by Henry James. Much of it made me think of the priest condemned for a long space to confess nuns.
—William Butler Yeats on Henry James

Jeffery Archer is proof of the proposition that in each of us lurks a bad novel. —Julian Critchley

Reading Joseph Conrad is like gargling with broken glass.
—Hugh Leonard

Just the omission of Jane Austen's books alone would make a fairly good library out of a library that hadn't a book in it. —Mark Twain

That insolent little ruffian, that crapulous lout. When he quitted a sofa, he left behind him a smear.
—Norman Cameron on Dylan Thomas

All that glitters is not cold.

· · · · ·

Gravity was invented by Isaac Walton.

· · · · ·

Greeks invented three kinds of columns:
Corinthian, Doric, and Ironic.

· · · · ·

GROWING UP THE TRELLIS WERE PINK AND YELLOW CONCUBINES.

· · · · ·

Henry VIII found walking difficult
because he had an abbess on his knee.

· · · · ·

If a pronoun is a word used in place of a
noun, a proverb is a pronoun used in place
of a verb.

· · · · ·

I'm not the kind of person who wears his
heart up his sleeve.

· · · · ·

Malapropisms Found
on Student Exams

King Alfred conquered the Dames.

* * * * *

People who live in Moscow are called
Mosquitoes.

* * * * *

Never look a gift horse in the mouse.

* * * * *

The squaws carried porpoises on their
back.

* * * * *

SALMON SWIM UPSTREAM TO SPOON.

* * * * *

Most people in the Middle Ages were alliterate.

· · · · ·

Brigham Young led the Morons to Utah.

· · · · ·

THE FIRST BOOK OF THE BIBLE IS THE BOOK OF GUINESSES.

· · · · ·

In the Olympic Games, Greeks hurled the biscuits.

· · · · ·

Wat Tyler led the Pheasants' Revolt.

· · · · ·

The patient had a deviant septum.

· · · · ·

SOCRATES DIED FROM TAKING A POISON CALLED WEDLOCK.

· · · · ·

Malapropisms Found on Student Exams

Rome wasn't burned in a day.

．．．．．

In the Bible, Jacob stole his brother Esau's birthmark.

．．．．．

Julius Caesar extinguished himself on the battlefields of Gaul.

．．．．．

Marriage to one wife is called monotony.

．．．．．

He always puts his foot in his soup.

．．．．．

King Harold mustard his troops before the Battle of Hastings.

．．．．．

THE POLICE SURROUNDED THE BUILDING AND THREW AN ACCORDION AROUND THE BLOCK.

．．．．．

HE WAS BETWEEN A ROCK AND THE DEEP BLUE SEA.

· · · · ·

The mountain range between France and Spain is the Pyramids.

· · · · ·

A leopard is a form of dotted lion.

· · · · ·

Money roots out all evil.

· · · · ·

Let sleeping ducks lie.

· · · · ·

The people who followed Jesus were called the Twelve Opossums.

· · · · ·

Let's get down to brass roots.

· · · · ·

Malapropisms Found on Student Exams

A rolling stone gathers no moths.

* * * * *

The Greeks gave winning athletes a coral reef.

* * * * *

Achilles' mother dipped him in the River Stinks until he became immortal.

* * * * *

THE BATTLE WAS WON DUE TO GORILLA WARFARE.

* * * * *

The store was closed for altercations.

* * * * *

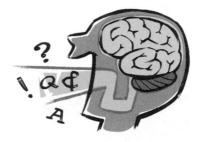

The liquid rose because of caterpillar action.

· · · · ·

To prevent head colds, use an agonizer to spray medicine into your nose.

· · · · ·

DON'T BITE THE HAND THAT LAYS THE GOLDEN EGG.

· · · · ·

It is beyond my apprehension.

· · · · ·

The amount of education you have determines your roll in life.

· · · · ·

Malapropisms Found on Student Exams

WE SEEM TO HAVE UNLEASED A HORNET'S NEST.

· · · · ·

Be sure and put some of those neutrons on my salad.

· · · · ·

Listen to the blabbing brook.

· · · · ·

He's a tough and remorseful guy.

· · · · ·

My new coat has lots of installation.

Overheard Linguistic Leapfrogs

You have to take the bad with the worse.

· · · · ·

The Iliad of Homer was not written by Homer, but by another man of that name.

· · · · ·

Abraham Lincoln wrote the Gettysburg Address while traveling from Washington to Gettysburg on the back of an envelope.

· · · · ·

Although the patient had never been fatally ill before, he woke up dead.

· · · · ·

William Tell shot an arrow through an apple while standing on his son's head.

· · · · ·

At least half their customers who fly to New York come by plane.

· · · · ·

Overheard Linguistic Leapfrogs

Before I start speaking, I'd like to say something.

· · · · ·

THE BLOOD CIRCULATES THROUGH THE BODY BY FLOWING DOWN ONE LEG AND UP THE OTHER.

· · · · ·

These hemorrhoids are a pain in the neck.

· · · · ·

The book was so exciting I couldn't finish it until I put it down.

· · · · ·

CONGRESSMAN SMITH STAYED AFTER THE TOWN MEETING AND DISCUSSED THE HIGH COST OF LIVING WITH SEVERAL WOMEN.

· · · · ·

The Gorgons had long snakes in their hair. They looked like women, only more horrible.

· · · · ·

The conviction carries a penalty of one to ten years in Alabama.

·····

During the Napoleonic Wars, the crowned heads of Europe were trembling in their shoes.

·····

The difference between a king and a president is that a king is the son of his father and a president isn't.

·····

FEMALE MOTHS ARE CALLED MYTHS.

·····

Fine furniture at reasonable prices: antique, colonial, and temporary.

·····

George Washington married Martha Custis and in due time became the father of his country.

·····

Overheard Linguistic Leapfrogs

The four seasons are salt, pepper, mustard, and vinegar.

· · · · ·

Athens was a democracy because people took the law into their own hands.

· · · · ·

Napoleon wanted an heir to inherit his power, but since Josephine was a baroness, she couldn't bear children.

· · · · ·

It's time to grab the bull by the tail and look it in the eye.

· · · · ·

THE JURY'S VERDICT SHOWED THEY WERE OF ONE MIND: TEMPORARILY INSANE.

· · · · ·

Lincoln's mother died in infancy, and he was born in a log cabin, which he built with his own hands.

· · · · ·

Magna Carta provided that no free men should be hanged twice for the same offense.

· · · · ·

The match was so close that it was hanging on a cliff the whole time.

· · · · ·

MOST OF THE HOUSES IN FRANCE ARE MADE OF PLASTER OF PARIS.

· · · · ·

The car had no damage whatsoever in the accident, and the other car had even less.

· · · · ·

One by-product of raising cattle is calves.

· · · · ·

You have to say about him, he doesn't mince his punches.

· · · · ·

The sacred cows have come home to roost.

· · · · ·

Overheard Linguistic Leapfrogs

She held out her hand. The young man took it and left.

• • • • •

The spinal column is a long bunch of bones. Your head sits on the top, and you sit on the bottom.

• • • • •

THAT SNAKE IN THE GRASS IS BARKING UP THE WRONG TREE.

• • • • •

He saw three other people in the restaurant, and half of those were waiters.

• • • • •

These hemorrhoids are a pain in the neck.

• • • • •

A virgin forest is a forest where the hand of man has never set foot.

· · · · ·

When they fought with the Persians, the Greeks were outnumbered because the Persians had more men.

· · · · ·

Bear to the Right: Questions Asked at National Parks

Is the mule train air-conditioned?

· · · · ·

Why did the Indians decide to live in Colorado?

· · · · ·

What time does the two o'clock bus leave?

· · · · ·

Can you show me where the yeti lives?

· · · · ·

How often do you mow the tundra?

· · · · ·

How much does Mount McKinley weigh?

· · · · ·

Did people build this, or did Indians?

· · · · ·

WHY DID THEY BUILD THE RUINS SO CLOSE TO THE ROAD?

· · · · ·

Do you know of any undiscovered ruins?

· · · · ·

How much of the cave is underground?

· · · · ·

SO WHAT'S IN THE UNEXPLORED
PART OF THE CAVE?

· · · · ·

Where are the cages for the animals?

· · · · ·

What time do you turn on Yosemite Falls?

· · · · ·

Was this [the Grand Canyon] man-made?

· · · · ·

[AT MOUNT RUSHMORE] CAN I GET MY
PICTURE TAKEN WITH THE CARVING
OF PRESIDENT CLINTON?

· · · · ·

· ·

402

[at Everglades National Park] Are the alligators real?

· · · · ·

Does Old Faithful erupt at night?

· · · · ·

How do you turn [Old Faithful] on?

· · · · ·

When does the guy who turns [Old Faithful] on get to sleep?

· · · · ·

We had no trouble finding the park entrances, but where are the exits?

Where Am I?:
Questions Tourists Asked at Visitors' Bureaus

Do you have a map of the Iditarod Trail?
We'd like to go for a walk now.

· · · · ·

Where can we find Amish hookers? We
want to buy a quilt.

· · · · ·

What is the official language of Alaska?

· · · · ·

WHAT'S THE BEST TIME OF YEAR TO
WATCH DEER TURN INTO ELK?

· · · · ·

Where are Scarlett and Rhett buried and
are they buried together?

· · · · ·

If you go to a restaurant in Idaho and you
don't want any kind of potato with your
meal, will they ask you to leave?

· · · · ·

I am trying to build a flying saucer. Where
do I go for help?

• • • • •

Where can I find a listing of jazz funerals
for the month?

• • • • •

WHICH BEACH IS CLOSEST TO THE WATER?

• • • • •

Have we made peace with the Indians?

• • • • •

VINI
VIDI
VIGI

Index

· ·

412

· ·

415